KINGDOM OF NIGHT

The Saga of a Woman's Struggle for Survival

Joseph Freeman

University Press of America,® Inc.
Lanham · Boulder · New York · Toronto · Oxford

Copyright © 2006 by
University Press of America,® Inc.
4501 Forbes Boulevard
Suite 200
Lanham, Maryland 20706
UPA Acquisitions Department (301) 459-3366

PO Box 317
Oxford
OX2 9RU, UK

All rights reserved
Printed in the United States of America
British Library Cataloging in Publication Information Available

Library of Congress Control Number: 2006927118
ISBN-13: 978-0-7618-3533-2 (paperback : alk. paper)
ISBN-10: 0-7618-3533-4 (paperback : alk. paper)

∞™ The paper used in this publication meets the minimum
requirements of American National Standard for Information
Sciences—Permanence of Paper for Printed Library Materials,
ANSI Z39.48—1984

CONTENTS

Foreword by Michael Berenbaum	v
Preface	ix
Acknowledgment	xi
Introduction	xiii

Part I: Before the Storm

Chapter One	3
Chapter Two	7
Chapter Three	15
Chapter Four	21
Chapter Five	25
Chapter Six	35
Chapter Seven	39
Chapter Eight	45

Part II: Auschwitz

Chapter Nine	51
Chapter Ten	55

Part III: Freedom

Chapter Eleven	67
Chapter Twelve	75
Chapter Thirteen	79
Chapter Fourteen	85
Chapter Fifteen	93
Chapter Sixteen	95
Chapter Seventeen	103
Chapter Eighteen	105
Chapter Nineteen	109
Postscript	111
Afterword by John K. Roth	117
Glossary	121
Sources	127

FOREWORD

Now it is Helen's turn.

Joseph Freeman is a Holocaust survivor from Pasadena, California, who for the past two decades has told his story in classrooms and universities, in writing, and in person throughout Southern California. I had the honor to meet him several years ago through my friend and colleague Professor John Roth of Claremont-McKenna College, whose writings on the Holocaust and the American dream have often touched my soul. John's friendship deeply enriches my life.

To meet Joe is to encounter a man now fourscore and seven who is bursting with energy and exuberant with a dedication and a determination to a cause. One can only imagine the energy he had a generation ago, for he is a whirlwind of activity committed to teaching and telling the story of what his generation endured, what so few of his contemporaries survived to tell, and what he rightly believes is so vital to strengthen the humanity and the decency of men and women, young boys and girls who are two generations and sixty years removed from the Holocaust.

Joseph Freeman is not struggling alone as he once did. In every community throughout the nation and every city throughout the world where survivors live we can meet such men and women. They are the backbone of the cause of remembrance, the spearhead of museums and memorials, educational centers and Holocaust curricula. Their deepest commitment is to fulfill the promise they made to those they left behind to remember and not to let the world forget.

Joe gives full credit to an inspirational speech he heard in 1978 by the exemplar survivor Elie Wiesel, who had written so eloquently of silence and paradoxically demanded of survivors that they speak—more importantly that they write. He also credits a post-midnight call from his son, then a student at Northwestern University who had heard a professor of engineering espouse the lines of Holocaust denial and who asked that he no longer be shielded from the truth so that he would be empowered to respond.

Many survivors have responded to the same call, at the same stage of life. They assumed this mantle of witness when they had reached the age where there are more yesterdays than tomorrows and when, often for the first time in their lives, they have the time and the strength to look back. Perhaps most importantly, they understand that what they say will be heard by a new generation; what they write will be read and appreciated. And they also understand—ever so deeply—that what remains untold, what remains unshared will never be known.

Together with his writing partner and friend, Donald Schwartz, Joseph Freeman has written his memoirs. But he did not stop there. He then wrote on the little known but deeply important chapter of the Holocaust, the death marches, the forced evacuations of emaciated and starved prisoners in the winter of 1944-45 from the concentration camps in the East—foremost among them Auschwitz—to other concentration camps. Prisoners were seldom given shelter or food as they walked through a frigid winter, often finding that the enemy was no longer the Nazis but death itself as they had to move beyond the limits of their own endurance and discover the inner will and determination to live. Joe gave voice to all those who shared his journey. As a survivor, he was in a minority of those who started out from the camps. Many—if not most—died along the way if they paused for a moment, if they weakened, if they slept too long or too little.

And now he has written his wife's story. Although titled *Kingdom of Night*, it should more appropriately be titled *Chaiale of Radom*, for she lived this story as Chaiale, the only girl in a religious family from Radom. The story begins with Chaiale's childhood. The daughter of pious Jews, she recalls a home of joy and comfort, a home blessed by spirituality and modesty, a home in which *Shabbat* and festivals were celebrated, education—at least for her brothers—was venerated, and where the quality of the Jewish community and their solidarity overwhelmed the antisemitism of some of her non-Jewish neighbors and even the occasional eruptions of the plague of East European Jewry: the pogroms. She loved all her brothers, but Fishel was her favorite. He was to become her savior as he rescued her from a forced labor camp and it is his absence that becomes a pervasive presence in the story that she narrated to her husband and was then told by Joe and Donald Schwartz to the world.

Foreword

One experiences the suddenness of the change. Survivors often chronicle their life in three stages—before, during and after—and Chaiale is no exception. "Before" is pre-September 1, 1939, the day that the Germans invaded Poland. "After" is May 8, 1945, the moment of liberation, when the war came to an end and a new, unending battle began to return to life, to rebuild after the devastation and to regenerate on a foundation of ashes in the shadow of the crematoria. "During" is the time of danger—growing danger.

Chaiale recalls the humiliation at the beginning of the war when one side of her father's beard is forcibly shaven, a humiliation that forces him to violate his religious faith by shaving the other side to preserve his dignity. She is candid as to how depressed the family became as the persecution intensified. In reading the depiction of the beauty of *Shabbat* before and the joylessness of the observance during their life in the ghetto, one gains a full understanding of how depressed her family truly became. However, as long as she lives with her family, and when after her rescue she returns to her family, she is not alone. The struggles that are endured together are no less severe but somehow less haunting to Chaiale.

She describes her separation from her mother. One Thursday in July 1942 Chaiale left her home. It was an ordinary departure.

"Mother, I am going for a walk and I will be right back."

"Be careful."

A truck stopped and that was the last farewell. Students may well relate these lines to the ordinary goodbyes by those who left their home in the New York area on September 11, never imagining that goodbye was farewell.

Her experience coincides with the history of her city, Radom. Being young and strong, she is selected for the work details and forced labor rather than deportation to Treblinka. But by 1944, even her work camp becomes a concentration camp. It was more than a change of jurisdictions, more than a change of attitude. It soon became the antechamber to Auschwitz. Young and able, she survives selection and is at Auschwitz for four months until she is transferred to Siemens Motors, which employed slave laborers to the very end. Chaiale describes the ties that bound one to life and the ties that endangered one's life at Auschwitz. She describes the hunger and the limits to which one would go to satisfy that hunger. She depicts—but does not condemn—those around her who traded sexual favors for food or clothing. Sheltered as the lone daughter of pious Jews, she was innocent and had not known men, had barely had contact with boys except her brothers and their friends. She did not abandon God even in God's absence, even when surrounded by the anti-God and anti-man at Auschwitz.

Her survival brought no joy, only the realization of what was lost. She returns home only to find a stranger living in her home, a stranger who bars her at the door. No return is possible. And so she searches for an aunt in Zamosc, a quaint Polish town. Her aunt survived the war masquerading as a non-Jewish beggar in Warsaw, and was permitted to return to her home and reclaim her business. She helps restore Chaiale as she leaves her hometown of Radom homeless, empty-handed and alone. Chaiale is reunited with one of her brothers and reunited with Joseph, Fishel's close friend, the man she first met in the camps and with whom she discovers emotions she had not known. She tells of the strange blossoming of what she learns is love. She is reunited with her surviving brothers who go to Dachau to mark Fishel's loss and again with Joseph, who soon becomes her husband.

Success in Germany follows, but it comes at a steep cost. Joseph and his bride must live in a land where the Nazis reigned for twelve long years and among people who surely embraced Nazism, even if they did not necessarily participate in the "Final Solution." So a new journey began to the United States, a new life and a new language, a difficult beginning and an even more lonely existence before encountering fellow survivors and before enjoying the fruits of their difficult labors. Life reestablished, children brought into the world, Chaiale—now Helen—had "survived survival," to use her words. And then, from 1978, the survivor became a witness, and in bearing witness she may have found the reason for her survival.

Surely, we who read her story must be grateful for all that she shared and grateful again to her husband Joseph, who again heeded the admonition to write and record and thus who brings Chaiale's story to the printed page where it will long endure. By telling of the "before" and "during," she has enriched the "after" and deepened the meaning of survival.

Michael Berenbaum
Los Angeles, California

PREFACE

So many years have passed. It is now more than fifty years since I came out from a living hell. Still the memories of my painful humiliation are a part of me. Sometimes I shake in disbelief. As a young Jewish girl I was exposed to the cruelest mental and physical torture. This I can never forget. Never again will Jewish life flourish in Poland, a country, which now stands as a cemetery for Jewish culture.

Jews have survived over the centuries thanks to our traditions and our way of life. The Christian world isolated us from the outside society, at times confining us in ghettos. Observing our laws and studying the Talmud was the most important element in our lives. We were the people of the Book and being isolated helped us to continue our traditional ways and to survive while waiting for the Messiah to come. Facing danger, our people always turned to the Almighty for help. Victimized by pogroms and plundering, our people offered little resistance while waiting for the miracle of deliverance. It took six million innocent lives to realize that as a people we have to help ourselves and then the Almighty will guide us on our way to overcome the danger and the injustice imposed on us. No more waiting for a miracle. We paid the price. The slaughter changed the mentality of our people.

A new generation was born in the shadow of that inferno. With the voices of their loved ones being tortured and murdered still ringing in their ears, there grew a will to refuse to give in to despair and a determination to stand up against the forces of hate and bigotry.

Professor Elie Wiesel said, "God exists where humans lived. In the Nazi's 'Thousand Year Reich,' humanity ceased to exist and so God's presence was not felt." But faith was not destroyed in the souls and minds of the half-alive moving skeletons. This belief in their Creator was the fever that burned so deeply in whatever was left of their failing bodies, reviving the vital spark of life necessary to overcome the Angel of Death.

ACKNOWLEDGMENT

No amount of appreciation can repay my debt to Peter Conveney for providing me with valuable suggestions in writing this book. Most of all, thanks to his encouragement, I continue to write.

Joseph Freeman

INTRODUCTION

Recalling my past is to relive my moments of despair. In some ways it was a relief to share with my husband, Joseph, the story of my degradation and moral pain. He, too, is a survivor, and I knew he understood how I felt. After we started sharing our tragic lives with the public, I understood the importance of reliving the horrors of our past. At the beginning, I could not hold my emotions. I cried. It took time to share my feelings with strangers.

For the past fifteen years, Joseph and I have addressed audiences with our moments of unrelieved pain and humiliation. We were two young Jewish souls lost in a world where death and terror, in its most barbaric and destructive forms, were imposed on a people deemed guilty only by the religion of their birth. Millions and millions of innocent lives were lost because of an individual who lived in a fantasy world, who tried to build an empire based on a theory of a supreme race. In the beginning, there were many who believed in the words of this sick-minded corporal playing the role of savior of a desperate nation. At the end, facing the overwhelming power of the Allied forces, he committed suicide, hoping to escape the hand of justice for the crimes he committed against humanity. He left behind his own nation—Germany— and a large part of the world in ruins and misery.

Why, you may ask, do I want to revisit my horrific experiences under Nazi barbarism? Why would I want to recall the inhumanity, the indecency, the incredible cruelty of what happened to me more than half a century ago? Because the Holocaust did not stop in Auschwitz. Despite what we should have learned from the past, atrocities have continued in the last half of the twentieth century and in the first years of the new millennium. By such atrocities as the ethnic cleansing in the Balkans and genocide in Rwanda, thousands died. Horrors and tragedies continue to occur though we are supposedly at the most advanced stage of human evolution.

I have fitfully lain in bed, hour upon hour, mystified as to why we humans repeat the mistakes of the past. I, who know what hunger can do to the human soul, cry out loud when I see pictures of little children—walking skeletons—who look identical to the inmates of Auschwitz some sixty years ago. Hasn't the world learned to combat misery and sickness? I know what it is to go on being constantly hungry, twenty-four hours a day. I know this feeling which many face again today. I cannot be silent. Maybe by my sharing my life, so full of pain, people will understand what bigotry and hate can do and raise their voices in protest.

My husband, who had endured unimaginable punishment in concentration camps, recognized the importance of recording his living hell. In 1996 he wrote of his experiences in *Job: The Story of a Holocaust Survivor* (Praeger Press), and again in 1998 with *The Road to Hell: Recollections of the Nazi Death March* (Paragon House). It was painful for him to go back in history, but he was able to do it.

For me, I found it almost impossible to write about my tragic past. I tried to and could not. Whenever I picked up a pen, my hands shook and I cried. I found it was easier to talk to Joseph about what happened to me. Only a Holocaust survivor, one who has lived through this kind of deprivation and personal humiliation, can understand my feelings of despair. Joseph went through the same hell, felt my helpless moments when everything was lost, when my mind wouldn't work, without hope in my heart.

But I had made my choice. I had to go back and suffer again. It took months—almost a year—before I could sit down with Joe and recall what happened so many years ago. Joseph listened and wrote as I related my story, a narrative often interrupted by tears. At times, I could not go on; I had to stop. But he encouraged me to go on, so that he could put my life on paper. It was an effort for him to use my words. As I opened my soul to him and relived those horrible moments of my past, I could see the tears in his eyes as he relived my physical and psychological torment. Despite my feelings of anger and pain, I continued my road back to the kingdom of night, recalling my life story, suffering again and again until I had finished.

I hope that the recollections that appear on the following pages can serve to instruct and inform readers of the consequences of hatred, bigotry, and intolerance; that, in some small way, it can help to make this a better world in which to live.

PART I
BEFORE THE STORM

CHAPTER I
YESTERDAY'S WORLD

I was born Chaja Borenkraut on September 2, 1921, in Radom, a city some one hundred kilometers (over sixty miles) from Warszawa, the capital of Poland. We were a large family, six boys and one girl. My parents worked very hard trying to support us. My mother had a little grocery store; my father owned a cooking oil factory. My grandmother also lived with us. My mother always left the house early in the morning and stayed at the shop until it closed. Coming home after a long, tiring day, she could not take care of me, and so this was my grandmother's job. My grandmother also prepared dinner for the family.

On Fridays my mother came home early from work to help my grandmother prepare the *Shabbat* dinner. One of her first tasks was to wash me in a big tub (we didn't have a bathroom), and then dress me for the Sabbath in special clothes. She also made my hair look pretty. After taking care of me, the boys had to be made ready for the Friday night dinner as well.

I never saw my mother resting. She was a workaholic, always doing something. She couldn't sit in one place—that was her nature. When she prepared the table for dinner, she would ask me to help her. I was always ready for the call. It was a routine for me. First, the white tablecloth; then, the large candleholder in the middle of the table. Next, the silverware and the beautiful dishes. My mother would always check to see that things were in their right places. Her last job was cleaning and polishing the wooden parts of Father's chair. Only after inspecting everything would she leave the room to change her clothes and put on her special wig for the Sabbath.

My father owned a factory that produced cooking oil, but he was also a scholar, a member of the Burial Society. It was an honor to belong to this organization, and very difficult to gain admittance. To qualify for membership, one had to spend years in yeshiva studying the Talmud and the Mishna, and gaining knowledge of the Jewish way of life.

To be accepted into the Burial Society, a man had to be known in the community and had to live up to a high moral standard. Then he had to pass a test before a special group of religious leaders. He also had to learn the ritual and the code of the Burial Society. After spending some time attending funerals and proving to the men in charge that he knew the rules, he was allowed to take part in burial activities. I remember, as a little girl, going with my father on some Saturdays and holidays to the society's house of worship. There, pious men gathered for hours meditating and interpreting the Talmud with the rabbi. They sat around the table for hours debating and asking questions. I would sit on my father's lap, and the people around us sang and had a good time.

Friday, at sundown, was a very special time, for it was only then that we all had dinner together. On that special day, father came home early and changed his clothes. He put on a black silk capote (a long jacket), black short boots, and for the Sabbath, a black hat. He always looked so distinguished. His short, dark beard, beginning to show signs of graying, framed his face and highlighted his dark eyes so full of life.

Before *Shabbat* dinner, father went to the synagogue. Only Herman, my oldest brother, went with Father, while the rest of the family waited at home. Upon returning, Father would step into the apartment, kiss the mezuzah, and loudly voice the greeting, "*Shabbat Shalom*" (peace in this house on the day of rest). We children sat around the table, waiting.

Nobody had the right to sit in Father's chair except Father. It was always ready for him whenever he was home. This was the rule in our house: respect for the head of the family. Father was always served first. After washing his hands, he would recite the blessing over the bread before taking the first slice. Mother took the second slice, Grandma next, then the boys and, at the end, me, the daughter. Sometimes, my father made an exception, turning to the sons with a smile (on holidays only) and saying, "Well, this time, Chaiale (my nickname) gets to go first. Remember always, boys, she is your only sister. Never forget it."

The Sabbath was a day of rest. The oil factory was closed and so was my mother's little grocery. Father went back to work Sunday afternoon, and mother opened the store from nine till twelve on Sundays. But Saturday was

Chapter 1 / Yesterday's World

not a work day. It was the time the family spent together. In the morning, Father went to the Burial Society's synagogue. The boys went with him. There they prayed until noon and came home for the Sabbath special meal. In the meantime, my mother, my grandmother, and I helped set the table.

Since on the Sabbath we couldn't warm our food, everything was prepared the day before. On Friday afternoon, my mother prepared a special dish, *cholent*, consisting of potatoes, barley, pieces of lean meat, to which she added water, onion, some pepper, and some salt. My grandmother took it to the bakery, where it was put into a warm oven to simmer overnight. Saturday, at lunchtime, my grandmother picked it up. This was the only warm dish at the Sabbath dinner. The stove, heated by wood and coal my mother put in Friday afternoon, kept the house warm until Saturday evening. Also a pot full of hot tea was prepared the day before, as no cooking of any kind was permitted on the Sabbath. The only light in our rooms came from a small electric bulb in the kitchen that was turned on on Friday and left on all day and night, and from a candle burning at the dinner table. The rules in our home were strict. And we obeyed them.

At noon, Father came back from the Sabbath service at the Burial Society. Following the meal that sometimes lasted for hours, Father spent time with the boys, listening to them, especially to Herman, who read verses from the Talmud. Father discussed with my brothers interpretations of the Bible. Herman was a student at the yeshiva and Father was very proud of him. Then the boys had to demonstrate what they had learned at their *cheder* (religious school). Afterward, father took a short rest. In the afternoon, he went back to the Burial Society to meditate and to listen to religious discussions, staying for the rest of the day.

The women remained at home while the boys sometimes went with Father. At sundown, he came home and performed the Sabbath-concluding *havdalah* ceremony. Father would light a candle with one hand and hold a cup of wine in the other. A box containing aromatic spices (sweet-smelling herbs, such as myrtle or cloves) was handed around for the entire family to inhale. The boys stood around the table while father sang a special melody in blessing and recited the prayers for the termination of the Sabbath. This ceremony served to emphasize the distinction between the sacred and the ordinary, the Sabbath (or festival) from the ordinary weekday.

My parents worked hard and enjoyed the Jewish way of life, not forgetting obligations to their family, their people and their tradition. And so, the respect and love we felt for our parents were the most important elements in our lives.

That was my home: surrounded by my family; sheltered from the outside world. We depended on each other in an atmosphere of tradition handed down for generations. Like many devout before us, we observed the Jewish way of life according to the Bible and the golden rules transmitted by the religious leaders of the Jewish community guiding our people in the millennia of living in the Diaspora.

Comfortable in this insular world, as a child I didn't feel or understand the hardships I would face in the outside world, especially what was required to adjust to the Polish population, many of whom were hostile toward Jews. But once I became of school age, that learning process soon began.

I began my formal education at a public elementary school for Jewish girls, four days a week from eight o'clock until two, and Fridays until noon. Twice a week a tutor would come to my home to teach me to read and pray in Hebrew. I was a good student and liked to spend time studying. My grandmother was always helping and checking my progress in Hebrew. For hours she would sit with me and listen to how I was reading, and she would correct my mistakes. By the age of twelve I already knew how to read and write Polish, Hebrew and Yiddish.

After elementary school I attended business school, where I started to read and write German. There I experienced the difficulty of being Jewish in Poland. First of all, the school was in session six days a week. For me, growing up in a very strict Sabbath observant family, it was impossible to attend school on Saturday. Luckily, the teacher was a very understanding human being. She made special arrangements so that I could catch up with the Saturday program in the middle of the week, in the afternoon hours. It was very hard for me, but this was the only way I could continue my studies.

CHAPTER TWO
THE PRZYTYK POGROM

There are specific moments in life that touch us deeply, moments we will always remember. In summer 1936, something happened that will stay with me as long as I live. I was fifteen years old, too young to fully understand the difficulty and the hardship that my parents had to face as Jews in Poland trying to raise a large family. But I did have a feeling of uncertainty and foreboding, constantly afraid that something unpleasant would happen to members of my family. Our parents used to tell us stories of the not-too-distant past, of pogroms and other attacks on Jews. We heard rumors, some of which turned out to be mere gossip and some which were true. One that I could not forget was the Przytyk Pogrom, a tragedy my family relived in great pain.

Rabbi Shapiro, a close relation on my grandmother's side, was the spiritual leader in Przytyk, a small town near Radom. He was the pride of our family. The rabbi was a fount of wisdom who was admired and respected by everyone who knew him. What a source of knowledge he was! My father always reminded us of what Rabbi Shapiro taught: "Never lose the belief in the Almighty. Trust Him. In time of despair, only He can help us."

The time of despair came on March 9, 1936. The position of Polish Jews had begun to worsen in May 1935 with the death of Jozef Pilsudski, a major force in the Polish government since 1918. After Pilsudski's demise, the Polish government gradually shifted toward a more authoritarian rule. Extreme nationalists were encouraged by the spectacular success of Nazi Germany, and violence against Polish Jews increased sharply.

In the winter of 1936 there were rumors that some radical nationalist group was planning to attack Jews. We were used to rumors, and some of us dismissed the warning as hearsay and mere gossip. But on March 9th, rumor became reality. In the middle of the night our sleep was interrupted by a knock on our door. My father answered it and there stood Rabbi Shapiro with a blanket over his head. I never forgot the frightful look on the rabbi's face. Afraid of being killed, the rabbi, was running away to save his life. He had escaped from his home in a horse-drawn carriage under a load of vegetables. There, in the middle of the night, stood God's servant in our doorway, shaking with fear. He kissed the mezuzah on the doorpost and holding on to my father entered our apartment. I can never forget the frightened look in his eyes when he took from his head the towel that hid his beard. Trembling, the rabbi clutched a prayer book to his chest. His head was covered with sweat. My father, with tears running down his cheeks, gently helped him to the sofa. He brought the rabbi a bucket with water and put a towel over his arm. The rabbi washed his hands and started to pray.

At this moment my grandmother took me gently by the hand into the next room. I sat on the bed, still shaking. Quietly I was thinking, why had they tried to kill a rabbi? Did he harm someone? Why did the Lord not help him? He was His servant. I was too young to comprehend what was going on. My grandmother explained what had happened. "My child," she gently said, "you have to remember, we live in a very dangerous world. You have to get used to being Jewish. Not to be ashamed. We are God's children. The Almighty will always protect us. Remember, sometimes you will have bad experiences that will touch you physically, sometimes mentally. Sometimes you have to act as though you do not hear what they are talking about. You have to learn to listen and not always to answer. Remember to get over sad things quickly. Remember not to act when you are angry. Just calm down. Don't forget that with the Almighty's help we lived through so may stormy and tragic events, and we survived. You saw, the rabbi came to us. The Lord was protecting him. Remember, the most important thing in your life is your family. We must support one another in the good times and also in the bad times. Only then can we manage and survive. This is also the rabbi's family—his home. Members of a family are always ready to help their loved ones in a time of crisis. This is our moral obligation, to help not only the close members of our family, but our neighbors, our friends, and friends of our people. You never know, maybe tomorrow you will be in need and someone will help you."

I was still confused, but my brother, Fishel, who was always looking

Chapter 2 / The Przytyk Pogrom

after me, made clear what was going on. He told me what had happened on that icy day in 1936. It was early; the morning sun was only beginning to rise. People were still half asleep. Some of the inhabitants of the Jewish area started to open the wooden doors to their houses, stepping into the street and looking to greet the day. With brooms they started to push away the snow covering the sidewalk. This was nothing unusual; townspeople always performed this chore in the morning. When they had finished, back they went into their houses. The city was slowly awakening to life.

Because of the rumors, Jews stayed away from the marketplace on this day and remained in their homes to avoid contact with the local peasants. In response to the anticipated threat, leaders from the Jewish town organization had complained to the higher authorities, fearing that the police would not interfere if some radical group should try to incite violence and disorder. They came away from the governor of the district with only empty words. There was nowhere to turn to for help. They came back home, disappointed, only to pray and wait for a miracle.

In the meantime, young leaders from Jewish organizations met secretly, debating the very serious situation. They knew they could not rely on the police for protection. They decided to prepare to fight, to defend themselves and to protect their loved ones and the members of the Jewish community in the event of an attack. They were determined to fight, to use any weapon they could find to defend against mob violence. Many of our people, however, mostly the Orthodox, took no practical steps to protect against attack. As they had done in past crises, they bowed their heads in prayer and placed faith in the deliverance of the Messiah.

But the leaders of the Jewish youth in this little town understood the gravity of the situation. They did not place their faith on the intervention of any religious redeemer. They decided that without police support it was up to them to fight and to defend the Jewish community in case of an attack.

It was quiet for a while. Peasants, now in the hundreds, began walking around in the market place. One farmer, seeking to buy bread from a Jewish bakery, was set upon by a group of hoodlums. That was the signal to start a riot all over town. A wild mob armed with pitchforks and clubs began to chase Jews calling out, "*Zabicz Zydow*" ("Kill the Jews") and "*Mordercy Naszego Boga*" ("Jesus killers").

Some of our people bolted the windows of their homes and businesses, but the rioting mob would not be deterred. Unruly throngs wielding makeshift weapons chased Jews into the streets, but there was one group of young Jewish people who were not running away. They started to fight, defending the lives of their loved ones. Like wild hungry animals, the mob began attacking these defenders screaming "Kill the Jews."

What happened next was entirely unexpected. A small group of bearded, elderly Jews joined the young in defending the Jewish community. Some grabbed steel bars from the attacking mob, hitting the hooligans with their own tools of destruction. The Jews fought back with such power and determination that the rioting mob slowly started to back up. This gave the defenders more courage to go on and not to let the attackers rest. The mob started to run away with Jews in pursuit. Some of the attackers threw away their weapons, and in panic and confusion, fled from the town.

At that moment, the police suddenly came out from hiding. They didn't like what they saw. The police began to protect the rioters; with revolvers drawn, they forced the Jews who were pursuing the attackers to return to the city. In the meantime, other Jews removed those who had been wounded at the beginning of the riot. It was quiet for a short time. The defenders hoped that the violence was over, that both sides had had enough. But the bloodthirsty mob could not digest the defeat. In a few hours the murderous Poles reorganized and, with the addition of thousands of peasants from the surrounding villages, they resumed their onslaught.

Thirsting for revenge, the lawless horde started looting and destroying Jewish property, clubbing whomever they found inside Jewish homes. Given a free hand by the authorities, the rabble ran after frightened children and women who had fled from their besieged houses. The air filled with the cries of children and women calling for help. This didn't stop the wild bands from running after the helpless trying to get away to safety.

In the meantime, attackers ripped nailed-down windows and doors from Jewish businesses. In a frenzy of plunder, they threw merchandise into the street as another group of marauders grabbed the loot and ran away. The ranting of "Kill the Jews" constantly pierced the night.

The town was littered with wounded Jews, many lying in the middle of the market place, practically afloat in a river of blood. But the bloodlust was not satisfied as rioters searched for new victims. A small group of defenders fought back. Suddenly, some shots were fired. One of the attacking hoodlums, Stanislaw Wiesniak, lay dead among some wounded Jewish youth and several bearded Jewish men. The news proclaiming that "the Jews killed a defenseless Pole" spread quickly.

Now the police, in force, joined the rampage, assisting the uncivilized bands in their job of killing, looting and destroying property. Whomever

Chapter 2 / The Przytyk Pogrom

they found on their way was mercilessly beaten. Still, the small group of Jewish defenders put up a heroic effort against the thousands of barbaric peasants. In the end, the police and the mob overpowered these Jewish fighters. The fighting subsided as the rampaging bands finished their criminal work. The police looked on while Jewish property was plundered, and then directed the looters to help them get away. Incredible!

The marketplace looked like a battlefield after a fight. The wounded, covered with blood, cried out for help that never came. The injured included Jews and their persecutors, lying side by side. This was Przytyk moments after the pogrom—a macabre landscape of broken windows and broken bodies strewn about. Clothing ripped into pieces littered the streets and alleys. Broken bottles were scattered on the frozen ground, their contents now forming an array of different colors of ice. Broken pieces of furniture left behind, all were evidence of the savagery of the vengeful multitude. Unbelievable! Like vicious beasts, they mercilessly killed their Jewish neighbors and friends of many years. This is what hate and bigotry can do.

But this was not the end of the bloodbath in Przytyk. Afterward, the police ordered people to remove the wounded and to clean the market. Order had to be restored after the pogrom was over. The mob, however, was not finished—there were many who called for yet more blood to be spilled. Still they sought more victims.

At the outskirts of the city, in a little wooden house, lived a poor shoemaker, Josef Minkowski, with his wife, Haya, and their four children. As a coda to the pogrom, the crowd of peasants attacked the poor Jewish family, killing the father and mortally wounding the wife and two of his little children. They butchered the shoemaker with axes, chanting, "*Zabicz brudnego Zyda*" ("Kill the filthy Jew"), while another group beat his wife. While Josef was lying in a river of blood, dead on the ground, one of the mob cut off his ears, holding them high and laughing, showing them to his friends. The beasts then grabbed two of the children who were trying to protect their crying mother, threw them into the air and impaled them with pitchforks. They lay unconscious in a corner with blood covering their little faces. Assuming that all were dead, the mob left them to finish destroying whatever was left of the house. The other two children who had been in hiding survived unharmed. Haya Minkowski and the two severely wounded children were brought to a hospital in Radom for treatment. Because Mrs. Minkowski had lost a lot of blood, it was impossible to save her. Though one of the seriously wounded daughters died, the other recovered.

I was crying as my brother related this horror. Again I recalled Rabbi Shapiro's words: "Never lose belief in the Almighty. Trust Him. In time of despair, only He can help us." The man who had said those words was now in my living room, shaking in terror. As a young teenager, I wondered how and if God could help us.

A group of wounded from Przytyk began streaming into our city. Upon learning of the pogrom, the Jewish community of Radom was in shock. Some members of Rabbi Shapiro's congregation joined him and stayed for a while at our house. I would listen to their stories, trembling in fear. For the first time in my life I felt the danger of living in the Polish community, my first exposure to the hate that burned so deeply in some Polish souls.

With great difficulty I started to comprehend the meaning of what had happened. Fishel would sit with me for hours explaining what was going on. He still believed that not all Poles hated us, and that we should feel proud that we were Jews. He introduced me to books on Judaism, and so I started to read the history of our forefathers. This opened a new page in my life. I was fascinated with the beliefs, traditions and experiences of our people. Fishel had an enormous influence on me; he implanted in me a desire to learn and a determination not to give in to those who would seek to oppress us. He loved me so much. He was not only my brother, he was my friend to whom I could turn to for advice at any moment. I loved him with my whole heart. He was someone I could trust, someone I could turn to for answers. He was always ready to help me.

When the bloodletting at Przytyk subsided, the Polish courts took over. But justice was not on their agenda. Influenced by national radical groups, the judges came down heavily on the victims of Przytyk. The courts officially denied Jews the right of self-defense. Fourteen Jews were arrested and punished for taking up arms against the assailants. Shalom Lesko was indicted for shooting and killing Stanislaw Wiesniak, one of the attacking Poles. Lasko and three other Jewish defenders were sentenced to eight years in jail. The remaining ten defendants received jail terms of up to ten months for defending their lives and the lives of their loved ones against the homicidal pack of Polish peasants. The Polish defendants accused of murdering members of the Minkowski family were set free for lack of evidence. The rest of the Poles accused of killing innocent Jews were given suspended sentences. These verdicts represented legal approval for acts of murder committed against the Jews by their neighbors, and sent the signal that further acts of butchery would go unpunished.

Chapter 2 / The Przytyk Pogrom

It was only in the Jewish press that one could find articles about the killings; reports of the massacre did not appear in Polish newspapers. Only the leaders of Jewish communities condemned the slaughter; it was only Jews who demanded protection of innocents' lives. But these were voices in the desert; the rest of the world seemed unconcerned about the plight and fate of Polish Jews. Undoubtedly, Hitler took note of this and remembered it very well.

This was "justice" in Poland in the year 1936. This was my world. These are the memories that I live with.

CHAPTER THREE
THE BEGINNING OF THE END

On Friday, September 1, 1939, Nazi Germany invaded Poland, and my life was changed forever. The war came at a time when I was only beginning to open my eyes, beginning to asking questions. Suddenly, my normal way of life was interrupted. German bombs hit the airport in our city; one explosive destroyed the building next to our house. This was the first time in my life I faced death, and it left me in shock. My mother and I ran away from our apartment, and for two weeks I was afraid to return home. I could not sleep, unable to erase the images of the people who were killed in the bombings. I was constantly crying; my world had fallen to pieces. It took time and a lot of persuasion from my mother until I returned home. Following orders from the Polish government, my brothers got to the other side of the Bug River as quickly as possible, where they met with other young Polish men to organize a defense of Poland. But without outside assistance, Poland could not stand up to the overwhelmingly destructive forces of the Nazi war machine. Although I did not know it at the time, the German invasion marked the beginning of the end of the Jewish population in Poland.

On Friday, September 8, the Nazis marched into Radom. Our father remained home that day, hiding in the house, afraid to leave. As part of their plan against the Jews, German soldiers were given a free hand to persecute the civilian population. They beat, kicked, and humiliated Jews in the streets, cutting off the beards of Orthodox Jews—amusing themselves at the expense of their defenseless victims. It was horrifying. Scared, we waited for the unknown.

Chapter 3 / The Beginning of the End

One morning, as my father went to work, he covered his face with a little hand towel so as not to attract attention to his bearded face. But luck was not with him that day and the SS caught him and cut off his beard on one side of his face. Himself deeply humiliated, it was also a devastating moment in my life, seeing my father step into our house, his face shaved on one side and bleeding. I started to cry.

This was the first time I had ever seen my father, who was such a proud man, in such a degraded condition. For a pious Jew to lose his beard, a symbol of his religion, was a calamity, a disaster. This was also a blow for my mother, who stood shaking, looking at my sobbing father. Never before had I seen my parents so distraught.

Silently, my father went to his room, closing the door behind him. I could hear his voice, praying to the Almighty. Although it was degrading for him to lose his beard, he removed the unshaved part of his beard to save his dignity. Afterwards, the times became even harder. After a few weeks my brothers returned home, exhausted. But the family Borenkraut was finally united. At least together we would face the violent tomorrows.

It was impossible to believe that people from an advanced culture, from a country that was the product of progressive forces in western civilization, could commit such unspeakable atrocities. When the Nazi nightmare began, my father explained to us: "Remember, we lived through an occupation by the Russians and by the Germans, and we survived. My father, your grandfather, was doing business with the Germans. This was during World War I. With the Almighty's help, we survived."

During the first month of the German occupation new laws were issued aimed at robbing the Jewish people of their property and depriving them of their civil rights. First, Jews were not permitted to attend public religious services. Then, the slaughter of animals according to Jewish law was forbidden. The next step was freezing bank accounts and taking over Jewish properties, which were then managed by a special government agency directly under the orders of the Reich's Finance Ministry in Berlin.

I was first frightened and then depressed over the changes in our lives. I was particularly devastated by the order to close all Jewish schools. I loved going to school and I loved books; I could not imagine how I could get along with my education interrupted.

The Nazi plan was to isolate all Jewish inhabitants from the surrounding environment. They began by restricting our movement. They excluded us from many public places, and allowed us to walk only on designated streets. Jews needed special permits to go outside, and very few permits were issued.

Chapter 3 / The Beginning of the End

All Jews over ten years of age were ordered to wear white armbands with blue Stars of David. Any Jew caught without an armband would be punished by death, often killed right on the spot. Also, any Jew would be beaten if he failed to remove his hat when passing a German in the street. Eventually, the brutality forced Jews to remain indoors; many ventured outside only to obtain food or medication, and even then they avoided main streets to avoid detection.

German soldiers and civilians arrived in Radom by the thousands to impose control over the city. During the first few months of the occupation, several thousand Jews from the Poznan and Lodz provinces were relocated to Radom. The occupation authorities began to requisition Jewish residences, starting with the homes of the richest Jews. They ransacked stores and warehouses owned by Jews and then levied a fine on the Jewish community to pay for the damage they themselves had caused. Restriction followed restriction. Jews were forbidden to pray in groups. The Nazis then looted our synagogues, boarded up the windows and then transformed our houses of worship into stables.

The High Holidays of 1939 came at the end of September. Yom Kippur, the holiest of days for Jews, became a day of humiliation and murder, resulting in the death of two worshipers. Regardless of the danger, however, Jews in Radom defied the Nazi orders and gathered secretly to fast and pray on that sacred day. My father prayed behind a wardrobe while the women sat silently, afraid that the brutes might search our apartment.

The silence was broken by shouts of *"Macht schnell schmutziger Jüde!"* ("Move quickly dirty Jews!"). From everywhere soldiers went from house to house searching for Jews who defied orders. A jackbooted officer found an old man with a prayer shawl and proceeded to punch and kick him relentlessly. The victim screamed in a hysterical voice, *"Eloheinu Melech Ha-olam hilf uns"* ("Our God, Creator of the Universe, help us"). Germans pulled Jews into the street by their feet, leaving broad swaths of blood on the sidewalks. SS men then forced elderly Jews on their hands and knees to scrub away the blood. The scene was straight out of a nightmare. Sadistic Nazis forced Jews to run in the streets with heavy metal beds on their shoulders. Those who could not keep up were pummeled with heavy wooden clubs. Someone pathetically tried to crawl and was clobbered by the butt end of a German rifle, becoming the first fatality on that Day of Atonement. One soldier tried to force a Jew to eat pork, but the Jew refused. Before long, the Nazi lost his temper and put a bullet in the head of the recalcitrant Jew. By the day's end, those fortunate enough to have survived the barbaric attack, returned to our neighborhood. They were in terrible shape—clothes torn, faces swollen and bloodied. The Day of Forgiveness became an evening of mourning for those so brutally killed.

After Yom Kippur, my father became extremely depressed over the restrictions imposed on Jewish religious customs and practices. Nevertheless, he prayed every morning. But I could see that he was deeply hurt. From then on, I never saw my father smile. He was forced to liquidate his factory because it became impossible to obtain supplies necessary to produce cooking oil.

Soon the atmosphere in our once happy home became morbid as we moved like shadows and communicated only in low tones. We lived constantly in fear, afraid of what awaited us. I missed the Friday night rituals, my father's blessings over the wine, and his prayers over the challah. We ate in silence, listened to sounds outside, ever ready to go into hiding when the sound of heavy boots came close to our door.

One morning, an SS man came to take my father to the police station on Peretza Street. I told my mother that I would go to the station and would very politely ask the German authorities to release Father. Unaware of the danger I faced, I was only concerned with getting my father out of jail. With a trembling fist I knocked on the door of the police station. As I entered, a uniformed German sitting behind a desk asked me what I was doing there. Sobbing, I said, "*Bitte, helfen sie mir*" ("Please, help me"). An elderly German entered the room and asked what was going on. I begged him for mercy, explaining that my mother was sick and that I needed my father to be at home. Tears streamed down my cheeks and the older man told the uniformed German to bring my father into the office.

When my father entered the room, I could see him trembling. "There must be a mistake, my father could not have committed any crime," I wailed. "Please help me." The elderly German looked at me and ordered the soldier to let my father go. He turned to me and said, "Take your father and go home before I change my mind." I thanked him, then grabbed my father by the hand and left the police station. My father did not say a word until we arrived at our apartment. As we entered the room, my mother, her eyes red from crying, ran to hug my father and thanked the Almighty for saving him. That was the first time I saw my parents embrace, as it was customary among the Orthodox for a husband to refrain from expressing feelings for his wife in public.

Chapter 3 / The Beginning of the End

Throughout that winter we waited helplessly for the unknown. I saw my mother age with each passing day. Neighbors disappeared with increasing frequency. At night we would hear voices in Yiddish calling out for help. Sometimes their pleas would be interrupted by gunshots and the crying would end. Some mornings I would look out the window and see Nazis grabbing people off the street and loading them onto trucks. My grandmother told me not to give in to despair. She assured me that the Almighty would protect us from the Nazis. But I felt myself engulfed by sadness and sorrow; I felt as if my growing up was suddenly aborted, as I could no longer do the things I so much enjoyed. I couldn't change my destiny; I was a Jew, and that was my crime.

Spring came but I could not enjoy nature's reawakening as I had in the past. In August some 2000 young men and women were deported to slave labor camps near Lublin. The wealthy paid other Jews to take their place in the deportation; the poor gave up their lives so their families would have money to purchase food. Our living conditions grew progressively worse in the fall and then the winter of 1941. My brothers found it difficult to get wood and coal, and food became more and more scarce. I found these hardships tolerable as long as my family was together, but that would soon end.

In the spring of 1941, all the Jews in Radom were forced to move into a ghetto. On March the 29th, two ghettos were established—one around Walowa Street (we lived on Peretza Street, the center of the ghetto) and a smaller ghetto at Glinice, on the outskirts of Radom. All Poles living in the area had to move out. The German Army then gave the Jewish population only ten days to relocate to the ghetto. But the area designated for the larger ghetto was already overcrowded with people, flooded with refugees from surrounding villages. And so the suffering of our community was compounded.

In the ghetto in Radom we were isolated, under the constant strict surveillance of the SS, the Gestapo and other Nazi officials. We had to go on living, but we could not overcome the brutal conditions in the ghetto. Without food, without medical supplies, with little hope, and no help from the outside, there was little chance of survival.

CHAPTER FOUR
THE GHETTO NIGHTMARE

Spring is the most beautiful time in Poland. But by the end of April 1942, one year after the Nazis had sealed the ghetto, there was little to celebrate. For those of us to be sacrificed on the altar of the Thousand Year Reich, oppressed by a Nazi regime in which right was wrong and wrong was right, it was still cold winter.

The sun did not shine for the twenty-five thousand souls in the Radom ghetto. Squeezed into a small area, scared, exposed to the most brutal treatment of the Gestapo and the SS, we lived in fear, not knowing what the next moment would bring. I was born at the wrong time and in the wrong place. I could not be the master of my destiny. But at least I was with my parents and siblings, which made it easier to face the hardship. For me, my family was my shelter, and being with them made me feel secure. I was young; my dreams did not stop. The sweet memories of my happy life before the catastrophe was my escape from my cruel reality.

My world before the war was the world of nature. I loved flowers. I liked to go to the meadows and just look at the earth surrounding me. This made me happy. But this was the world that now ceased to exist for me. In the early days of my incarceration, I would run to the wire fence to gaze at the trees and flowers just beyond the ghetto. Flowers did not grow in the ghetto.

Staring at the beauty of nature made me feel good. I would push my face between the openings in the wire fence and close my eyes for a moment. I was in yesterday's world, now forbidden to me. For seconds I was back in the meadows with Fishel, running around, relishing the beauty of Mother

Nature. I was happy, laughing, trying to catch some butterflies. The voice of my brother rang in my ears. But the wires of the fence pressed against my face, cutting deep into my skin, bringing me back to dark reality. Tears flowed, filling my eyes. In front of me, outside of the ghetto, life was going on. The sun shone. But in our place of living hell the sky was filled with dark, heavy clouds. The sun did not shine for those condemned to death. For us it was a foreboding night without an end. I felt like a little bird in a cage, moving my wings, trying to fly into the open sky but unable to escape. Nevertheless, as long as I was with my family, I had hope. Maybe we would survive this hell. My father was always reminding us, "If we as a family stick together, helping each other, it will be easy to survive and to overcome the hard times." He had no way of knowing what lay in store for us.

Though the Nazis were using our men, they were still short of the manpower needed to keep their machine of destruction going. Every day they would scour the ghetto and conscript able-bodied Jewish men as slave laborers, ground meat for their war machine. Men too old or unable to work were targeted for death. Increasingly, the Gestapo compiled names on lists and entered the ghetto in search of those people. When they found them, the Gestapo would kill them in front of their families. They would then quickly go on with the searching and killing of others.

Grabbing people in the street became routine. The SS came in groups, followed by trucks. We knew the vehicles were there to gather men and remove them from our midst. And so, at the moment the trucks passed through the ghetto gates, there was panic in the streets. People ran for cover in cellars and other hiding places. The police, made up of Jewish men selected to blindly obey Nazi orders, assisted in rounding up the men whose names were on their lists.

Not terrorized enough during the day, at nights we were even more frightened. Our sleep was often interrupted by the sound of shots. We would arise from our beds in shock, not knowing where the gunfire was coming from. We listened and waited. It would be quiet for a while. Then came the sound of heavy boots running on the steps of our apartment house. On whose door would they knock? Who would be next? Sometimes, the sound stopped. This was a relief. But when the sound of marching soldiers came closer and closer to our door, we waited in dread. The men always slept with their clothes on, their shoes in their hands, in the event of the fatal pounding on the door. When it came, my father and brothers instantly jumped out of bed and into their hiding places behind the wardrobe and the wall, places so small the men could barely stand. The demanding

Chapter 4 / The Ghetto Nightmare

knocking at the door was followed by loud voices. The guttural command, "*Aufmachen, schnell!*" ("Open, quickly!") still rings in my ears. It was so many years ago, but recalling it now still leaves me shaking.

It was terrifying when the Nazis eventually banged on our apartment door. I was sitting at the table pretending that I was fixing my clothes. My mother was beside me with a basket full of clothes. Although my heart was beating fast out of control, I was frozen in fear. My grandmother called loudly in German "*gleich*" ("right away"), making noise with the keys as she moved toward the door. Quickly, the men disappeared behind the wardrobe. As my grandmother opened the door, the Nazis pushed her away, shrieking loudly in German, "*Wo sind die Männer?*" ("Where are the men?"). My grandmother was silent. The Germans then searched from one room to another, looking around. My mother told them that the men were at work.

Everything happened so quickly, but it seemed like an eternity for me. As fast as the soldiers had come in and looked around, they left. Then there was a moment of relief. Still shaking, my mother came close to embrace me. The danger was over for a while. A tapping on the side of the wardrobe and the men started to come out from hiding. My younger brother, Abraham, was still trembling. Mother embraced him and kissed him. With her arm around him, she gave him something to drink. Then, she put him to sleep.

Sometimes, at night, either lying in my bed, or sitting up, while my brothers were asleep, it was hard not to sink into the depths of despair. I was just twenty-two, feeling alone as I faced my brutal oppressors, the SS. But even then, I tried not to lose hope.

This was a typical night in the life of my family, one of many filled with pain and anguish. Although our family survived that night of terror, in a short time I would be alone in this brutal world.

As the Germans continued to cut the supply of food, hunger began to make its mark on the inhabitants. People moved silently, like shadows. The Nazis cut the ration of food again, not enough to survive. The situation became desperate. To ease conditions, the Jewish leaders in charge of the ghetto set up a large kitchen where free soup was served daily. Still too little nourishment, too much misery. Then came the raids which so often interrupted the activities in the ghetto. People ran wildly about, trying to escape the brutal treatment at the hands of the Nazis. To add to our distress, it became increasingly difficult to buy food from the Poles, as the SS checked everyone entering the ghetto gates. Anyone bringing in food was punished severely. It became harder and harder to merely survive.

Day passed into night, summer into winter. Helpless, we went on living without hope. Shortage of medication was another problem. Because of the terrible conditions, people sickened, victims of starvation, tuberculosis, overcrowded conditions. Then typhoid broke out. Despite the lack of medicine, the staff at the overcrowded hospital worked hard, regardless of their safety, putting their lives on the line. Some of them contracted the disease and died. Still, the doctors and staff worked day and night, trying their best. But there were too many; sick people died by the hundreds.

Before the Jews were squeezed into the ghetto, the Nazis had confiscated all modes of transportation; consequently, there was only one horse and one carriage to transport the sick to the hospital.

It was under these conditions that we went on living . . . and dying.

CHAPTER FIVE
THE GATE TO HELL

One day passed after another in the ghetto. The constant tension, not knowing what was next, made me apprehensive, afraid and concerned about the safety of my family. I worried how I would take it when the moment came that I would have to face the loss of a loved one. Especially on my mind was my mother. I felt so helpless, knowing that she was crying on the inside. What could I do to help her? Even after so many years, I can still see her lovely, beautiful face. But the constant stress took its toll: She aged years with every passing day. It was torture for me to look at her.

But as long as my family was together, it was possible to endure the hardships. I felt moments of despair, yet I still had hope that we could survive. Then, in an instant, it all changed. It was Thursday, noon, late in July 1942. "Mother, I am going for a walk and I will be right back." I remember those words. Those were my last words to her. Her answer still rings in my ears. "Be careful. Watch where you are going."

My mother always worried about my safety. I was not far from my house, walking to the corner of Peretza Street and Walowa. Unexpectedly, a truck stopped. Two SS men quickly jumped off and grabbed me by the arms. A third lifted me, screaming in German, "*Schnell, in Lastwagon*" ("Quickly, into the truck"). They threw me into the back of the truck, and I landed hard on its wooden floor. The SS men then pulled down the back cover. It was dark inside; I could hardly move or see. In a short time, the truck was filled with other Jews. I was in shock. I felt so helpless I could not even think. It had all happened so quickly. Tears streamed down my face; I was afraid something terrible was going to happen to me. Did they grab me to kill me? Were these the last moments of my life? I knew that not many came back when the SS took them from the ghetto. But maybe, I thought, I will be a lucky one who will survive. Who knows what the devils will do to me? Then I remembered my grandmother always telling me, "Never lose your belief in the Almighty. In danger, the Lord will help you. He will protect you." I silently started to pray. "O Lord, help me. I am lost. You are the only one who can protect me. My life is in your hands."

I sat on the cold, hard bed of the truck, sobbing, shaking my head back and forth. Then the vehicle suddenly lurched forward. Where were we going? I didn't know. The truck increased its speed. Looking around, I noticed that the back cover was not fastened tightly so as the truck picked up more speed the cover loosened, letting in some light. I was then able to see the women and men in the truck with me, sitting quietly, holding their arms around their chests. They moved back and forth as the truck sped along. Unexpectedly, a voice called "Hela." I turned my head and there, next to me, was Mrs. Gertner. Her husband was a family friend. She quietly talked to me, trying to cheer me up. After a short drive, the truck stopped. An SS man lifted the truck cover and ordered us to step down, telling us not to worry, that they needed women to work in a German-owned establishment.

My nerves began to calm, somewhat. I recognized others in our group—Bella Buch and her husband. The Nazis had also abducted them. The SS led us to a large building with a sign in German, indicating that it was a construction company. They then brought us into a kitchen where every morning we had to help with serving breakfast to the employees. Following breakfast, we had to clean everything in the eating hall and then sweep the walkways. At lunch, we followed the same procedure, helping to serve and then cleaning up in front of the office. We always had some supervision while we continued our work. We were warned that we would be severely punished if we tried to escape.

We were then taken to our living quarters. The women had a big room for themselves, whereas the men were housed in another building. Against the walls were wooden beds covered with blankets; there was also a table and a sink with one faucet from which poured only cold water.

Although I knew Mrs. Gertner, Bella Buch, and her husband, I felt horribly alone. Looking around the room, I could see I was not the only one who was afraid. All of us were in shock. After a while, an SS man returned to take us to the kitchen, where he ordered the cook to serve us some food. This was my first meal away from my loved ones. I could

Chapter 5 / The Gate to Hell

hardly swallow. I was hungry, yet I choked on every bite I put into my mouth. It was very hard for me to come to terms with what was happening to me.

My first night away from my loved ones was torturous. I could not sleep. For hours I lay quietly on my bed. From burning and sweating, my body would suddenly be freezing. Shaking from cold, I would then be sweating from waves of heat that swept over me. I cried, feeling lost and alone. When I closed my eyes I saw my mother's face, covered with tears. But her voice lacked the sweet intonation that always soothed me, and the look in her eyes filled me with dread. I cried out aloud in my sleep and woke up sobbing. Mrs. Gertner came over and embraced me. I could not hold back the tears. It seemed just yesterday that I had been at home with my family, and now I was desolately alone in a strange and foreboding place.

I began my first day of work at six o'clock in the morning. After cleaning the kitchen, we stopped for breakfast: a cup of hot water and a piece of bread. Then it was back to work, cleaning the walkways around the kitchen. It took us a few hours to remove the debris that had accumulated outside the buildings. The SS men constantly had their eyes on us while we worked. When we finished, it was back to the kitchen to clean the dining area, to get it ready for lunch. Our work was not too hard and with the ration we were getting it was possible to survive.

A short break—lunchtime consisted of a cup of soup and a little piece of bread. A brief rest, then back to work. I could not free my thoughts from despair. Yesterday I had been with my loved ones, now I was a nobody, a slave. Every time a German passed by I trembled in fear that he might harm me.

My first working day ended at five o'clock in the afternoon. Four of us went to the kitchen, bringing back bread cut into pieces along with preserves and some hot coffee. An SS man came to our room to remind us to do our work, not to worry, and to assure us that no harm would come to us. I listened, but I could not be consoled. It occurred to me that this was my first Friday night away from my family. Alone, exhausted, I sat on my bed. Closing my eyes, I was back home. Oh, how I missed my family! I imagined the table ready for the Sabbath dinner, with my father saying the prayers over the wine, then the blessing over the challah. I forgot where I was, so sweet were the memories. And then the dreaded thought entered my mind: Would I ever see them again?

The nights at the construction company were especially painful. Although I could hardly keep my eyes open, I could not keep my mind from racing. I was consumed with thoughts of how to find the strength to cope with the rapid changes in my life, how to find the strength to endure the hardship without the support of my parents and siblings. Because of this I was only able to sleep for a few hours, leaving me exhausted and listless at work cleaning the kitchen, sweeping the streets.

The sleepless nights and monotonous days wore on me, making me wonder if I would ever escape my hell. I tried to convince myself that my family was still alive, but something gnawing at my consciousness told me that I would never see them again.

I had been working at the construction company for a month when the SS man came into our quarters, ordering us to get ready to leave for another *Arbeitslager* (work camp). Following our morning ration, we were loaded into a truck and put on our way to a new labor camp.

I will never forget the name Wolanow, the place where my true hell started. We had been on the road close to an hour before arriving at a complex of buildings in an open area surrounded with guards. We saw people working in the nearby fields. Just months earlier, Russian prisoners of war had worked in Wolanow, but those who hadn't died of starvation were then killed by the Nazis. As part of the Nazi program of making Poland *Judenrein* (free of Jews), Wolanow then became a labor camp for Polish Jews rounded up from nearby Radom. The women were housed in barracks inside the camp, the men in a complex of barracks outside the camp.

In the beginning, there were few restrictions. I could move around although I was not allowed to leave the camp. I met some people from Radom—Lola Scheinfeld and her family, Renia Zajac, and Cerale Gutman—which made me feel somewhat better. These were people I knew growing up.

Myself and some women from the building company were assigned to the same room. Also, one girl, Rose, was already in the room when we came in. She had been with us in the other camp. Rosie had been initially transferred from Szydlowca, a Jewish village that had been liquidated as part of the Nazi plan to concentrate Jews into larger population centers so as to make them easier to control.

There were six women assigned to each room. Everyone slept in wooden beds. Because it was harvest time, I worked with a group of women to help farmers outside the camp. It was not so bad as the farmers sometimes brought us food and sometimes invited us to their houses. We even had the opportunity to exchange some things for food.

The first weeks working in the fields lifted my spirits; I was grateful to be in the open air, surrounded by greenery. The trees were full of fruit,

Chapter 5 / The Gate to Hell

ready to be harvested. It relaxed me. This was the world with which I was familiar and comfortable: the world of nature. But this ended when the harvest was completed. After that, we were assigned to work in shops repairing uniforms for the German Army.

Each day, after a breakfast consisting of a small piece of bread and watery coffee, we would leave the camp for work in the shops. We stayed at our workstations until the evening, when we trudged back to the camp, escorted by Jewish policemen. When we got back, we were given some soup and again a piece of bread. After work, we could move around.

As time passed, I became friends with Rose. Things at this point were not so bad—the work was not hard and as long as it was warm, it was possible to survive. But toward the end of autumn, the weather changed. We had to walk to work in the rain, without warm clothes. Returning from work in wet clothes to cold rooms made many of us sick. We would lie awake at night shaking from the cold. It was especially bad at night; there were no toilets in the quarters, so we had to run outside to the restrooms and then back.

At that time of the year in Poland there was a lot of rain. Before long, a typhoid epidemic spread quickly throughout the camp. With little food and no medication, the situation grew worse with each passing day. Fearing that the epidemic would spread, the SS decided to close down the camp. We were quarantined and not allowed to leave the compound. The SS walked around the place with arms, guarding the gate to insure we could not get out. Outsiders were not permitted near the camp either. Isolated, we waited for the unknown. Then the SS cut our rations. Now, not only did we have to face the cold, but also the shortage of food weakened us further. We had one doctor—Przytycki was his name—who did his best under impossible circumstances. Helping the sick infected with typhoid with no medication was not easy.

Now we were a parade of sick people, supporting one another, moving very slowly, like shadows. It was torture, quivering from the cold and hunger. The sneezing and coughing, mixed with the voices of the Jewish police trying to keep order, depressed us even further. It took a while to get our rations, but immediately after receiving mine I ran back to my room to devour the meager portion. I began to doubt that I would survive.

Every morning the SS forced us outside, hollering loudly in German, *"Schnell, schmutziger Jüde!"* ("Quickly, dirty Jews!"). Afraid, we ran out into the frosty, damp open. The cruel soldiers would then shoot into the air, herding us like wild animals, pushing us against each other. Those who could not maintain their footing fell onto the soft, swampy ground. But we could not stop; we had to jump over the ones on the ground. Then the SS pushed and squeezed us into a small confined area where we were forced to stand, pressing together, hungry and shivering. Afraid, we held on to one another. After about an hour, the SS forced us back into the barracks. They had fun, enjoying what they were doing. This was play for them, taking advantage of the scared souls among us.

Then the Nazis suddenly changed the routine. Entering our quarters screaming and ranting, they went from room to room, looking for sick inmates. You never knew if you would be next to be dragged away by the murderers. Some of us were still in good health and sat around the table fixing some clothes, pretending to be busy. It was such a terrible, depressing condition. I don't know where I got the energy to go on and live from one day to the next.

Then my friend, Bella, caught typhoid. What a terrible sickness it is. It leaves you like a child, helpless, unable to physically function. Without medication there was no help for the sick. This is one of the reasons the epidemic spread so quickly. The sick lay constantly in their beds, coughing, sneezing, and crying for help. It was a mad house. At night the crying and noise from those infected was so loud it was impossible to sleep. Still, the healthy tried to help the sick ones. But not for long. The epidemic spread quickly.

My condition changed the moment my friend who had been sleeping next to me caught typhoid. She was holding on to me. Sick and alone, her husband could not help her. The men had been confined to their barracks. I was deeply touched when she cried in a delirious voice, "Help me, help me. Don't let me die." It was very painful to look at her in such agony. But I was young and strong, and I did not think I would catch the disease; I was convinced I could take the hardship of looking after her.

She was on fire. The high fever changed her drastically. Sometimes I could not understand what she was saying. She was helpless, like a little baby. For twenty-four hours I cared for her, washing her face, applying a wet cloth to her forehead. When washing her sweet face she recognized me. She clutched me, calling my name and pleading every few minutes, "Help me, help me." Her delirious voice still rings in my ears today; I cannot forget it.

I stayed many nights taking care of my friend, not sleeping. I was going on and on until I, myself, began getting weaker and weaker. At the end, my system gave in. First, my head felt like a piece of very hot stone. Then my body was on fire and I could not sleep. I lost my appetite and was

Chapter 5 / The Gate to Hell

constantly thirsty. One moment I was shaking from the cold and the next I was perspiring, lying in a river of sweat. It became impossible to hold on. I felt that my end was nearing. What could I do? I was alone and sick. The only ones who could move around were the Jewish police who came into our quarters. I got a hold of a policeman by the name of Kampel. I had known him for some time and had invited him to our house in the ghetto a few times. I asked Kampel if he would deliver some letters I had written to my brothers in the Radom ghetto. I did not know what had happened to my brothers, whether they were dead or alive. The idea to write came at the moment I felt that my struggle was coming to an end. I had lost my physical strength and my mind did not work. The writing was an attempt to say goodbye to my loved ones before I faded away. I could not take any more. The fever was making me crazy. I wrote that my brothers should keep together and help each other to survive. I finished the letter by letting them know that I loved them and missed them. I asked them to tell Fishel that I missed him the most.

From that moment on I do not remember what happened to me, but when I opened my eyes I saw my brother Fishel. Maybe I was dreaming. I stretched out my hand and called "Fishel!" and then passed out. When I awakened I was lying in bed, surrounded by my brothers. It had taken three weeks to recover from my terrible illness.

When I felt better Fishel told me how I had survived. He shared with me the worries, difficulties and dangers to which he had been exposed trying to get me out of the Wolanow *Arbeitslager*.

As I had requested, Kampel got in touch with my brothers and delivered the letter I had written. At that time, Fishel was working for the German *Wehrmacht* (army). It had been evening, as he was returning from work, crossing the gate into the ghetto, when Kampel approached him. "Fishel, I have a letter from your sister, Hela."

Fishel told me, "At that moment I was in shock. I did not know where you were. I grabbed the letter, asking aloud, 'Where is she?' His answer was, 'In Wolanow *Arbeitslager*.' My hands shook trying to open the letter. I started to read and began crying. Yes, this was my sister. Every written word was a knife cutting into my chest. I ran home. Morris, Sam and Jacob were already home. I stepped into the room proclaiming, 'Hela is alive. I have a letter written by her.' I read the letter, crying. When I came to the sentence, 'When you will receive this letter, I will probably be dead.' I could not read any more. It touched me so deeply.

"When the Nazis kidnapped you from the ghetto our father said to me,

'Fishel, remember, try to find out where they took Hela. Maybe you can help her to be together with you. Please promise me.' I promised I would do whatever possible. 'Remember,' I told father, 'this is my only sister and I love her, too.' So when I read your letter I hit my fist on the table shouting, 'Our sister needs help. I am the only one who can help her. I can move around. Now, it is late. In the morning at my work place I will talk to my friend, Corporal Miller. Maybe he will help me.' The night was a long one. It was torture for me. I was lying in bed, thinking how you were suffering without help, so sick and no one around you. I knew I had to act quickly, otherwise I would lose you.

"At that moment I closed my eyes and I saw your beautiful face covered with tears, constantly calling my name, 'Fishel, wherever you are, help me.' It was so painful for me. I love you so much. I was ready to do the impossible to help you. Finally, the morning came. I went to work and talked to Miller, who was in charge of our group working for the army. I told him I needed his help. Whatever he needed for himself or his family I would get. The price was a pair of boots for him and shoes for his family. That was possible for me to get, so I agreed. Soon, in a military truck, I was on my way to the camp. Before leaving the city I made a stop at the ghetto. I asked Kampel to come with me. I, too, paid him. Nothing is free; money had always helped as long as we had been living in the ghetto. Rich people had been bribing the Jewish police to replace them with poor souls to do the hard work. At the working places, the German supervisors also took bribes. They just looked away when the rich people dealt with the *kapos* (Jewish camp functionaries) who had been getting them out of the ghetto so they would not have to work hard.

"Kampel was a big help in getting me into the Wolanow *Arbeitslager*. Once inside, I went straight to the building where you were. I brought with me a gold watch, some gold chains, and money. It was dangerous, but I didn't care. I was just thinking of a way to save you. I remember the moment I stepped into your room; your eyes were closed, your face covered in sweat. You were making some kind of noise I could hardly understand. Then you moved your head, opened your eyes wide, and stared at me for a few seconds. You started to cry out loud. You recognized me. In a whispered voice you said, 'Fishel, help me.' It touched me so deeply I began to cry. But there was no time to lose. I had to act quickly.

"In the meantime, Kampel spoke to the chief of the Jewish police who was bribed to help us. He found out the best time to get you out would be when the guard was changed at the gate entrance to the camp. We got you

Chapter 5 / The Gate to Hell

ready with the help of some of the women in the room and waited for the signal. I gave the gold watch, two gold bracelets, and a bundle of money to bribe the guard at the gate. As the chief of the Jewish police spoke with the guard, walking to the side with him, Kampel and I carried you quickly out of the camp and placed you into the truck. It only took seconds. Once in the truck we were on our way to the ghetto. We did not have any difficulty getting in through the gate into Sziptalna Street and straight to the hospital. Dr. Szenderowitcz, at this time, was an elder of the ghetto and also in charge of the hospital. Since he knew you, a bed was made ready right away.

"But this was not the end of your suffering. Someone reported us to the SS. It was in the evening when I brought you to the hospital. Late that night the SS came in with the Jewish police and ordered us to the ghetto police station. To escape from an *Arbeitslager* (work camp) was punishable by death. You were lying on a bench with a high fever and I was standing beside you. We waited, not knowing what the Nazis would do to us. Then fortune smiled upon us. In charge of the ghetto at that time was *Stürmbahnführer* Bloom. It was his daughter's wedding day and, consequently, he was in a good mood. He might have ordered our death but instead he returned you to the hospital. For the first two nights I was in your room, watching over you. I left the hospital only after I was certain your condition had improved."

There was a shortage of medication in the hospital, but I had a clean bed and it was quiet. Being removed from the mad house in Walonow and the presence of Fishel helped me a lot. The rest helped me overcome my sickness. After two weeks, Fishel took me home to recover. But I could not function by myself. Helpless, I needed someone to be around me constantly. The Bornstein brothers lived next door and one of their relatives, a middle aged woman, offered to help. She stayed and slept in the same room with me; she was like a mother to me. Wherever she is, I wish her the best.

Still, it was very dangerous for me to stay in the ghetto to recuperate. Fishel knew that and together with the chief of the Jewish police made arrangements to protect me if some *aktion* were to take place. Naturally, Fishel had to pay some money to provide for my safety.

I listened quietly while Fishel told the story of my rescue. I cried. I kissed him, and said, "I owe you my life. You risked your life to save me."

CHAPTER SIX
LAST DAYS IN THE GHETTO

The clock didn't stop. One month came, then another. Summer passed into fall. Slowly I recovered and regained my strength. Being with my brothers, especially having Fishel around, left me feeling more secure. But being confined to my room for so long, I didn't know what was going on in the ghetto. My brother had shielded me from the terrifying reality that faced the remaining inhabitants of the Jewish community. And so, the moment I stepped out into the streets I became depressed. I saw our people moving without life—shadows, silent, without purpose, their frightened eyes just wandering around, afraid of the unknown.

Abek Fried, my brother's friend, was the head of the Jewish police in the ghetto so we always knew ahead of time when an *aktion* would take place. One day a Jewish policeman informed Fishel that the SS were at the ghetto gate looking for men to work. People soon were running for cover and in just a few seconds the street was empty. I stood there shaking. Fishel then pulled me by the hand, urging me to run to our apartment. Once there, Fishel told to me not to worry, that as long as we were in the ghetto we were safe. But still, I had to face a harsh reality. Three thousand condemned souls, the leftovers from the Jewish community in Radom, were squeezed into a small area, trying to live despite intolerable conditions.

With every passing day, I began to feel stronger and stronger. I also started to go outside to visit friends. I felt alive again, and slowly my mind started to work. With the passing of time, I gained some weight. All the symptoms of my sickness disappeared. Fishel, always at my side, did not leave me alone for a second.

We went for short walks, always alert for signs of danger. I liked to go to the wall surrounding the ghetto at Swarlikowska Street, to stare through the opening between the bricks, savoring the greenery, the trees, and the flowers. It made me feel good. Closing my eyes for a second, my soul transcended the ghetto wall. I tasted the freshness and the sweet smell of nature. But when I reopened my eyes I was reminded that I was still in a living hell.

Cut off from the outside world, we were like caged birds stretching our wings, unable to fly out free into the sky. My mind reached through the hole in the wall where life was still going on. On one side of the ghetto wall was death and starvation; on the other side life did not stop. I saw children far away playing and laughing. Behind me, in the ghetto, our children were dying. In the morning some of them would be found dead, lying on the walkways, still holding fast in their stiff little hands a piece of bread. At last they were free. No more pain—their little souls on the way to heaven. The Angel of Death was the master of our destiny. Exposed to the most cruel torture and savage behavior, we were prisoners with nowhere to go. A ghastly cloud hovered over our place of misery. Silently, I prayed to the Almighty, asking why do we had to suffer so? What was our crime? Wiping the tears running down my cheeks, I turned around and stepped back into the world of condemned souls.

Poland in the fall of 1943 was warm, pleasant and so beautiful. The leaves were changing their color to yellow and from far away it looked as though someone had painted them in gold. This time of year I loved to go into the garden with Fishel and collect the brilliantly colored leaves lying on the ground. But that was in the past. In the present, we weren't human anymore. We had been turned into robots, blindly obeying the orders of the masters.

On November 8, 1943, the small ghetto in the city of Radom was liquidated. On short notice we had to assemble on Szwarlikowska Street, facing the gate to the ghetto. I was about to leave our apartment when Fishel called me to wait and to close the door. He gave me a little bag with some jewelry. "Keep it. We never know what will happen with us. Wherever we will be sent, or if we are separated, you will have some jewelry to buy some bread. It will help you." I started to cry. "How about you? You, too, can use them. Why give them to me?" I said. But Fishel insisted, "I can always handle wherever I will be. Remember, you will be alone. I will be together with our brothers. It will be easier for us to face the hardship than for you. Take the jewels; there is no time to argue. Keep them."

Chapter 6 / Last Days in the Ghetto

Tears flowed from my eyes; I could hardly see. I could not understand what was happening. Is this good bye? My head was on fire. I didn't know what to do.

With his words ringing in my ears, he extended his hand with the little bag toward me. "Take it and hide it." I grabbed it and stuffed it into my brassiere. Without another word, Fishel ran down the steps and then into the street. People were running, shoving one another, trying to avoid the Jewish police who were hollering, pushing people, forcing them to move faster. It was the first time I saw living little children in the ghetto. There were not too many, but those who had survived thus far had been in hiding. Saving children cost a lot of money, as the Jewish police had to be bribed to look the other way. Now, mothers held their little children as they ran, pressing them to their bodies.

Soon Szwarlikowska Street was packed with the last survivors from our community. Compressed like sardines, it was impossible to move. I stood close to Fishel, holding on to his hand. We waited and waited, every minute an eternity. Some children started to cry; some people prayed silently. Frightened, sweat poured down my body. Fishel, sensing my terror, tried to cheer me up, telling me not to worry.

Shaking, raising my eyes to the sky, I prayed to the Almighty to save us. Suddenly there were loud voices from all around us, roaring "Move, move fast!" Terrified, people pushed ahead, forcing the ones in front of the line to move. Some started to cry, some prayed. The wailing of the children still rings in my ears even after so many years. Then the SS and the Ukrainian guards in front of the gate moved in, calling loudly in German, "*Schweigen. Mach schnell!*" ("Silence. Move fast!"). They started to hit those making noise. Afraid, the crowd passed through the gate, silently moving out into the street, just looking around on our way to the unknown, still uniformed as to where we were going.

The Polish inhabitants of the city stood on both sides of the street, staring silently at us, as we were forced out of the city. For two hours we marched under the constant surveillance of the SS, the Ukrainians, and the local police, thereby making escape impossible. Finally we reached our destination: the Szkolna barracks complex. Fishel whispered, "This is a labor camp where Joseph's brother, Isaac, lives and works in the ammunition factory. Don't worry, I will take care of you. We managed in the ghetto. Remember, you have five brothers around you. As long as we are together it will be easy to meet the hardship. Let's hope for the best."

CHAPTER SEVEN
SZKOLNA LABOR CAMP

Slowly we entered the gate to our new place of misery. A group of SS with their Ukrainian cutthroat helpers watched the hopeless souls passing before them. As we trudged by they ripped away whatever we had in our hands, especially our bundles, which they cut open in their search for money, jewelry and valuables. Everyone went through this awful, humiliating personal search. The Ukrainians even forced some of our people to take off their coats. Spreading the coats on the ground, they tore away the linings in their search for hidden items.

Finally, we we were ordered to halt in our new camp, Szkolna *Arbeitslager*. From the main road we could see a complex of barracks, where we would suffer but, perhaps, survive. For the majority, however, exposed to starvation, cold and sickness, many would perish.

Immediately, the women went to the left and the men to the right. The main road divided the women's sleeping quarters from the men's. We had some restrictions, but for the time being we could move around. In the morning we each were given a cup of coffee and a piece of bread. As in the ghetto, the Germans ordered men and women to work as slave laborers. Most of us were forced to work in the ammunition factory, but some were assigned to other shops located within the camp's boundary.

At this time, the Jewish police, under the leadership of Cheil Friedman, the *Lagerelder*, were in charge of assignments. With these people, Fishel knew his way around. Because in Szkolna it was possible to buy a good working place, in the morning he came to my barracks and told me to get ready. He had paid a lot of money and I was going out of the camp to work in a *Bekleidung* (clothing) warehouse. The *kapo* in charge of our group was Usher Goldberg, who was also my brother's friend. I was given a job as a clerk, taking care of orders brought in by Wehrmacht and SS. It was a large building. On the first floor was a huge supply of clothes. I could not believe what I saw in the basement. There, in front of me, was a mountain of furs that the Nazis had confiscated from the Jewish population, furs they now used to make warm clothes for the soldiers fighting in Russia.

At the warehouse I truly began to realize how Jews were exploited as a means of keeping the German machines of destruction rolling. The possessions they took from us weren't enough. Now I discovered that after they murdered our loved ones, and before burning the bodies, they ripped off wedding rings, in most cases by cutting off fingers. The Nazi monsters also forced inmates to pry open the mouths of the dead for the purpose of extracting their gold teeth. The gold was then melted and used to purchase raw materials for the German war machine.

In the warehouse I had to take care of orders brought in by the Wehrmacht. I was also in control of the inventory and had to write a daily report. All in all, I kept very busy. One morning, the *Untersharführer* (quartermaster) in charge passed by. He politely asked me if I would be willing to help his wife at his house. This was the first time a German had asked, not ordered me to do something. I had grown accustomed to Germans hollering loudly, using force, inflicting pain and suffering on our people, but in front of me now I saw a gentle human soul.

The quartermaster asked me to come work in his house to help his wife by minding his children in the afternoons. They had two beautiful children, a boy and a girl and I found that she talked to them in a gentle caring way. He had told his wife about me, and when I arrived I found her to be as pleasant as he was. She showed me unusual respect and invited me to dine with them, but I felt uncomfortable sitting at a table in a German house. I would listen to him speak, but was afraid to open my mouth. Yet the way she addressed me was reassuring and made me less frightened.

They asked me to play with the children and watched how I handled them. They then told me they approved of me and said I had the job. I would come from the factory and find the children waiting for me to play with them. They were happy youngsters, especially Helga, the little girl. Now I had two jobs: one at the warehouse and one in the quartermaster's house.

But life was very harsh at the camp. Each morning we had to quickly dress for work. Our morning ration consisted of a piece of bread, sometimes jelly, and a cup of a hot, black solution they called coffee. Then, we

Chapter 7 / Szkolna Labor Camp

assembled in groups, according to the places where we worked. A Jewish policeman stood at the head of each group as we waited to be counted by the *Lagerelder*. Then we were marched out the gate to work. The same procedure was followed upon our return to the camp, after which we lined up for our evening ration: a pot of warm soup and a small piece of bread. Sometimes, on Sundays, we were treated to a little piece of salami. After "dinner," we were allowed to walk around until eight o'clock, when we were confined to our sleeping quarters.

One morning I was ordered to prepare four hundred furs for the army. We had to work really fast to meet a two-week deadline. Some women helped me tear off the lining material of the furs that were then cleaned and made ready for shipping. As we did the work I discovered that the material we were removing from inside the furs was being thrown away. I thought this was wasteful. I told Fishel that the discarded cloth could be used to make winter clothes. "Bring one over and let me see," he said. "Maybe you are right. But be careful."

Being winter, it was cold, and we were without warm clothes. The next morning I went to the *Untersharführer*'s office and asked if I I could use the undercoats that were being thrown away in trash barrels. I got an okay. Going back to the camp, I took only two overcoats, putting them under my skirt and blouse.

Fishel examined the ripped material and realized that he could exchange it for food. At his work place he came in contact with Poles to whom he sold the linings from the furs. Sometimes the Poles would pay in food and sometimes in money.

Fishel and I found other ways as well to help us survive. One day I went to work wearing a pair of shoes that belonged to Fishel. I exchanged them for military boots I had found in the warehouse and in this way my brother had good shoes. Leather was a very important commodity because it could be used for many purposes. Every day at work I would take military belts which I rolled tight around my waist. I would bring these strips of leather into the camp and exchange them for food. Some of my friends fashioned short coats from the leather. I was also able to take socks from the warehouse for my brothers and me. It was possible to pilfer these items with relative ease since I was in charge of inventory. My survival and the survival of my brothers depended on such ingenuity.

Joseph, Isaac's brother and Fishel's close friend, was especially ingenious. At this time he was working in the maintenance department as an electrician at the Waffen ammunition factory. He befriended his foreman, a Pole, which enabled him to move around the plant. In the meantime, Isaac worked as a dental technician at an SS medical office and would often be paid with bottles of vodka. Vodka was highly desired by Poles, who could not get it because of wartime rationing. Isaac gave Joseph the bottles to exchange for smoked meat, salami, and cheeses from the Poles he met at work. The foreman, who looked after Joe's security, got a bottle of vodka for free.

Joseph's inventiveness enabled him to smuggle the food into the camp. Wearing wide trousers, he constructed a little contraption of strings to hold the food in special little bags. Passing the gate, he lifted his arms into the air. As the police searched his trousers, the little bags, tied around his waist, slid easily to the front of this coat. Turning around and putting his arms down, the little bags slid up without any noise, easily passing the search. Once inside the barracks, Joseph had a special little corner where he cooked eggs, hamburgers, and spaghetti, which he then traded for valuables the prisoners had hidden. The system worked beautifully: the foreman was happy, the Poles were getting the vodka and leather they could not buy outside, and we got the food needed to go on living. Such inventiveness was the only way we could survive under the brutal conditions at Szkolna.

One evening, Fishel came in to let me know Joseph had invited us to dinner. We went to the temporary barracks where Isaac had a little room to work and sleep. I was astonished by what I saw. There in the barrack was a table with a pot full of meat dumplings floating in a steamy, tasty sauce. There was a basket full of fresh rolls, and in the middle of the table was a small brisket cut into pieces. For a moment I forgot where I was. I felt alive and happy for the first time in recent memory. Staring at Joseph, I felt strange. In Joseph I had found someone with whom I could share and talk freely, someone besides my brother. For a second I thought, is this love? I was afraid; something inside my heart was saying, "No. No. This is not the place, not the time. You are not ready. Facing the unknown, you could not find a place in your heart for someone to love. You have enough worries. In this hell you can find only a friend. You are waiting your whole life for this moment, but it came at the wrong time. You cannot dream about a shiny tomorrow facing the cruel reality of today. Only death awaits you; there is no place for a sentimental feeling. My body, so young, felt the yearnings of physical desire, but my head said no!

I closed my eyes for a moment, trying to think, when Fishel's voice brought me back. "'Are you tired?' he asked. I answered, "No. No. For a

Chapter 7 / Szkolna Labor Camp

moment I was thinking, why have we been deprived of our rights? What did we do wrong? What crime was committed? Now we are spending a few short moments, forgetting the misery and the endless hardship destroying our souls. I always worry about your safety. Now Joseph shows up—another friend and another worry. It is so hard for me."

My brother interrupted quickly, "Remember, so far we have had luck. As long as we are together, we must do our best to find a way to beat the inhuman Nazis. We have not lost hope. You never know. Maybe we will survive."

This was Fishel—always cheerful, building up my spirits, urging me not to give up, to go on facing the hardship and believing we could survive. But that night the time passed too quickly. Happy moments, I will always cherish and remember them.

Our conversation was soon interrupted by a knock on the door. "Eight o'clock, curfew time," the guard called out.

Back in the barrack I could not sleep. For hours I lay on the wooden board with eyes open, thinking: I am so young, but I have already seen too much in my short life. I do not have the pleasure to dream. I was in my teens when the German brutes forced my family and me into the ghetto. The notion of loving someone besides Fishel had never before come into my mind. Yes, I was young, but the hardship and the abnormal way of life had aged me. I was constantly fearful for the safety of my loved ones. One worry was enough for me. I could not afford the luxury of even thinking about falling in love, of being with someone to share my dreams, of planning for a future. I was not free. I was part of a herd of sheep, following blindly, pushing ahead, moving, but not thinking. My soul was afraid of the unknown. How could I possibly fall in love?

CHAPTER EIGHT
MY STRUGGLES AT SZKOLNA

The routine at Szkolna was excruciatingly monotonous. Morning rations, lining up to work, returning to camp with pieces of leather hidden under my skirt, evening rations, curfew, and to bed. Once a week I worked at the *Untersharführer's* house. At one point some inmates asked me to help them get some uniforms so that they could try to escape. I asked Fishel what to do.

"It is up to you," he told me. "But remember not to put yourself in danger."

"No, it isn't dangerous for me," I reassured him. "I can easily bring uniforms out piece by piece."

Each day I left the warehouse with pieces of clothing hidden under my skirt and, in a short time, they had their uniforms. A few days later Fishel informed me that their escape was successful.

Things changed dramatically in January 1944, when overnight the Szkolna Camp turned into *Katzet Lager* Radom.

Specially trained SS men who had previously organized and supervised concentration camps in Lublin took over our camp. Immediately they built a double barbed wire fence around the camp. Watchtowers were erected in each corner and in the middle of every fence. The SS, with loaded machine guns, kept a twenty-four hour watch from their high towers, constantly alert to strange movements, ready to act.

I felt terrible. Our movements were now even more restricted than before. Even more distressing, the behavior of the *Kapos* changed under this new regime. Many of the *Kapos* were once inhabitants of the same city, people we had known our entire lives. Now they were practically indistinguishable from the SS—beating and tormenting us. They were following orders from their new masters, but the unexpectedly harsh treatment from former friends and neighbors was sad and depressing.

Led by *Lagerelder* Friedman, the *Kapos* gathered us at the *Appelplatz* while other *Kapos* searched our barracks for those who were missing. Screaming and pushing, they lined us up five in a row, forming a square around the assembly place. Then Friedman, satisfied that everyone was in line, issued an order in Polish, "*Uwazaj zdem czapki*" ("Attention! Hats off"). He then reported to Hecker (the SS officer in charge of the *Appel*), who would then report to *Hauptstürmführer* Sigman, the camp *Kommandant* and now master of the destinies of the last habitants of the city of Radom. The report was double-checked with office records, which took hours and hours while we stood at attention in the *Appelplatz*. I can still see the faces of the older women who fainted and died from exposure. They'd lie there on the ground until the counting was over. The torture of the *Appel* ended only upon a signal from the *Kommandant*.

Slowly the SS tightened their grip on us. Ukrainian guards constantly patrolled around the women's sleeping quarters, separating it from the other sides of the *lager*. Confined to our quarters, it was no longer possible to leave the barracks after curfew. Even the activity of the *Kapos* was limited to keeping order at the lines we stood in to get our rations. The only way to get into the women's barracks was through bribing the Ukrainians. A bottle of vodka was the price for a few minutes, otherwise there was no more visiting time.

Once Joseph came in for just a few minutes. We had no privacy. He did not kiss me, as he conducted himself in the proper manner in which he was brought up. Traditionally, East European Jews found a mate only through a matchmaker. It was a very strict way of life. For a young Jewish man, a girl was reachable only in dreams and books. He might feel romantic, but to kiss a girl took time. Joseph was part of the post–World War I generation of Jews hungry for new knowledge, eager to explore new possibilities. But it was not easy to break from centuries-old traditions.

In March 1944, some three or four hundred men and women were suddenly selected by *Lagerkommandant* Sigman and taken to the railroad station. From there they were sent straight to the ovens of Majdanek, one of six death camps built by the Germans in Poland. The following day, Fishel informed me that Isaac, Joseph's brother, went with the group

Chapter 8 / My Struggles at Szkolna

to Majdanek. He told me that Joseph was working at the ammunition plant and thus had avoided the *aktion*. That was the last time I heard any news about Isaac.

Soon it became more difficult to smuggle items back from the warehouse, since the SS searched everyone returning from work. Now I could bring in only one piece of leather at a time for the Jewish shoemakers who were our steady customers. Shoes were very important since without good shoes you could not survive the harsh Polish winter. Fishel and I were lucky to have soldier boots; others had worn-out shoes that had to be repaired. Some prisoners still had money to pay the shoemakers, who then paid me for the leather I supplied.

Conditions in the camp worsened with every passing day, but visits from Fishel lifted me from my malaise. Just thinking that he was not far from me gave me hope to go on.

Spring came and went. We, the doomed, could only pray to the Almighty to give us the strength to meet the hardship. That was all that was left: a faint spark of hope in the hearts of the condemned souls.

That summer I saw the mood change in the house of the *Üntersharführer*. His wife had packed their things, as if getting ready to move. He, too, was nervous. In July 1944, German soldiers from the eastern front—wounded and in very bad condition—came to our camp. Bitter from defeat, they loosed their anger and frustration upon us. I was confined to the barracks, no longer permitted to leave the camp for work. The inmates at the ammunition factory were also ordered to stop their work and were sent back to the barracks. The nights were very scary. We could not sleep. The sound of Soviet cannons interrupted the silence of the night. Shaking, we listened, fearful the SS would finish us off before facing the powerful Red Army advancing from the east. It was no secret any more. We knew what was going on.

Afraid of the Soviets, the SS guards packed their belongings in preparation for evacuation. Many of the possessions they had accumulated had been looted from Jews in the liquidation of Radom. Now we saw how they hurriedly tried to save their skins by sending the stolen property with their families to Germany. Some of us hoped that the SS would disappear and that the Red Cross would save us. Unfortunately, the Nazis had other plans for us.

On orders from the camp *Kommandant*, the *Lagerelder* instructed the *Kapos* to ready all inmates for evacuation the next morning. Our hopes shattered, we waited, not knowing where we would be going. Then, in a rush, the SS started to destroy the evidence of their brutality. The morning came and we were run out by the *Kapos* and assembled for evacuation. By the end of the day, the last surviving member of the Jewish community left the city of Radom, ending a culture of hundreds of years. Radom was officially *Jüdenfrei* (free of Jews).

PART II
AUSCHWITZ

CHAPTER NINE
THE ROAD TO AUSCHWITZ

We moved out from our camp, a column of exhausted, hungry, skeletal figures and marched through the city of Radom that not too long ago had been my home. Now I was leaving, taking with me memories of happier days—so short—of my youth.

I will never forget that march as long as I live. The city—and a culture—lay devastated, a community of thirty-five thousand people erased forever. Not a sign left. The hate-filled brutes had burned our books, destroyed our places of learning, our cemeteries and our houses of worship. Not a thing was left, only ruins. Every sign of Jewish life had disappeared, leaving the vanished community only a vague memory. I looked back for the last time, at the houses that remained. They had not changed, but the city, now *Jüdenrein*, had been altered forever.

On our Via Dolorosa we passed through the streets where we had once lived, now inhabited exclusively by Poles who silently watched the parade of Jews leaving their city forever. In the distance we could see a column of sick people from the *Ambulatorium* (the so-called hospital), squeezed into uncovered horse-drawn carriages, on their way to the same fate that awaited us.

As we continued on the road for several hours, with the SS watching us closely, it became increasingly more difficult to go on. Some prisoners started to move out of the lines. At this moment, armed guards, with guns pointed, ran at them, hollering loudly, hitting them and pushing them back into the lines. All of us were very frightened.

Despite the danger, those of us physically strong enough continued to help those too weak to move on. But time was working against us. With every passing hour we became weaker and more exhausted. Despite unbearable heat, we continued to go on marching for hours. Soon it became dark. The first painful day of our journey had come to an end. At nightfall, we moved out from the road into an open field. In the ever-increasing darkness I could still make out a sign: Walanow. I remembered the name of the place where I had worked after being kidnapped by the SS. From a distance, I recognized the barn where Polish farmers had hidden some food for us.

A helpless feeling began to take hold of me. I sat in the field dreading the unknown that was coming. My fellow prisoners and I were tired and hungry; some of us had faces covered with blisters from the day's burning sun. We sobbed in low voices trapped inside our exhausted bodies. I gazed at the night sky wondering why I was made to suffer so. I had not committed a crime, but I was suffering as though I had. Why, Lord? I am so young and miserable. Why me? Why do days full of pain and misery still await me? I had to bite my lip to go on.

Tired, I finally fell asleep, but not for long. Voices of the ranting SS awoke me. The guards forced us to move out, hitting those who responded slowly to their orders. From afar we must have looked like an army on a march, but in actuality, we were a wretched band of the doomed. The new day brought a burning, brilliant sun. In the blistering heat, there was no water provided us. As the day progressed, the dust from the road made breathing difficult. Soon, the older people could not take anymore. And the cries of children mixed with the wailing of those calling "water, water" made the SS furious. They struck the stragglers with the butts of their guns.

As we struggled along, the SS forced the column to move to the side of the road in an attempt to avoid cities and people. We passed some villages, where peasants stood idly by refusing to help us, just staring as the parade of skeletons passed by.

Thirst is the worst punishment to which a human being can be subjected. When some prisoners noticed rainwater that had collected in ditches at the side of the road, driven by thirst they broke from the line and ran toward the ditches. They were immediately shot by the SS and left there in pools of their blood. Passing the bodies of our friends, some of us silently recited *Kaddish*, the prayer for the dead.

After pushing our tired bodies all day, we settled in an open field for another night of temporary relief. Fortunately, I had good shoes, but some people could not march further because of blisters on their feet. Fishel came over to cheer me up. I felt better, knowing I was not alone. A friend,

Chapter 9 / The Road to Auschwitz

Majer Cyna, came to my side and asked me to escape with him and his elder brother Dudek. I was conflicted; should I go with them and leave Fishel, the one who had put his life in danger to save me? No, my love for my brother was stronger than my desire for freedom. What will be, will be, I told myself. I am not alone. I will stay with my brother. That was the end of it.

Majer and his brother dug a trench in the ground and covered themselves with a layer of soil. At daybreak, the SS again began running us from our resting place, and soon we were back on the road, our third day on our march to the unknown. Luckily, the SS did not detect the missing brothers, both of whom survived the war.

Eventually, the SS ordered us to halt when a truck loaded with potatoes came to a full stop near the column. We descended upon the vehicle like hungry animals, devouring as many potatoes as we could. Two days without food and then only raw potatoes on empty stomachs, swallowed too fast, made us sick. Forced to push ahead, crying in pain, rubbing our bellies with trembling hands, we continued the march, but some people just couldn't make it. Some inmates stumbled and the SS beat them and forced them to stand up and go on. Others gave in entirely, unable to move. The cruel murderers then killed them and dragged them to the side of the road, a warning for us not to stop.

Though we recognized that we were condemned to death, we still pushed our tired bodies ahead in slow motion, barely moving. Still, even in pain, we held on to each other for support, so that the weak could continue on the journey. We were a bedraggled mass, a disorganized throng crawling along the path to our doom. The blisters on our feet made it feel like we were walking on nails. Regardless of the pain, the blisters, the parched lips, we wretched souls stumbled on, biting our lips with each small step. The constant pain and the heat left us unafraid of being hit by the vicious beasts who tormented us.

Turning my head, I realized that the horse carriages with the sick people were gone. They had disappeared without a sign. The Nazis had driven the sick and the elderly into the woods and had killed them. The empty carriages soon returned to the column and began to collect those who had dropped by the roadside. Soon, a fully-loaded carriage moved toward the woods, where the passengers were again quickly disposed of.

I cannot remember exactly how long we were on the road, maybe a week or less, but every moment was an eternity. The SS killed sixty or more of our friends. Still, we were determined not to give in to these killers.

As we marched, the SS again tried to prevent us from moving through some little villages, but it proved impossible as we were in a very populated part of Poland. Once, an old peasant woman holding a wooden cross with a holy picture approached the SS men. She clutched the cross to her chest and had banners of red, white, gold and blue flying high in the air behind her. It was an unforgettable picture: An old peasant confronting the SS, not afraid of being killed by the murderers. In Polish mixed with German words, she warned the bestial Germans to stop the slaughter and atrocities. They tried to drive her away but she resisted and kept calling after them. Unfortunately, she was the exception. Most Polish peasants simply stared at us from both sides of the road, seemingly happy to be finally rid of the Jews.

Looking around, I tried to find Fishel, but could not locate him. Suddenly, I feared I would never see him again. I was devastated. Not myself anymore, I became part of a desperate mob, running wild, confused and disoriented. I did not care anymore. I started to call out loudly, "Fishel, Fishel." I did not know what to do; I was in a panic.

Soon we were forced into a dark building, stuffed like sardines, pressed one to another. I started to cry. I sat, frozen, not moving, with my eyes closed. The air was heavy with sweat and stink from the tired and dirty. I could hardly breathe. It was easier to take hardship as long as I had my brothers, but now I was alone. Yet the will to survive was still strong in me. I knew I had to face the unknown with the help of the Creator. Maybe, maybe, I would yet live. So far my angel had watched over me.

I passed out and when I came to bodies were close around me, pushing and in horror-stricken voices screaming, "Bread, bread." The live shadows were now standing up and frantically pushing one another, racing for the small scraps being thrown to them. I could not comprehend where the pieces of bread that were flying through the air were coming from, but people in the darkness were fighting over them. People with outstretched hands over their heads fought and pushed in their attempts to catch the meager sustenance. I was hit with a small piece of bread and quickly grabbed it, holding it tightly to my chest. No power could take it away from me. I ate my morsel very slowly, taking over an hour to devour it.

CHAPTER TEN
AUSCHWITZ: A MONUMENT OF MANKIND'S BESTIALITY

"The horrors of Auschwitz have become legendary, and the name itself has passed into international usage as a byword for all that is bestial in mankind." (Encyclopedia of the Holocaust)

After a week or so on the road, we arrived in Tomascow, a small city to the east of Krakow in southern Poland. The SS marched us to a railway terminal where we were pushed into boxcars, women separated from men. There was no time to think. The SS stuffed as many people as possible into every car, then slid the heavy doors shut. We had no idea of where we were going.

With a lurch, the train started up as we struggled against each other in the cramped car. We were so tightly packed that there was no room to fall down. During the trip armed guards with machine guns watched us closely. A Nazi stood on the roof of every car, ready to shoot in case someone tried to escape. A few SS men watched us from a specially built boarded compartment inside the train.

Squeezed and leaning on my fellow inmates, I could hardly breathe, though air came through a little opening high on the side of every car, an opening covered with barbed wire. I cannot recall how long we were in the boxcars, but every moment was filled with suffering. Some women started to cry. The smell of urine mixed with the odor of unwashed bodies. Many of the women were unclean, and the odor from menstruation was overwhelming.

Chapter 10 / Auschwitz

After several hours, the train stopped. It was August 6, 1944. In the early morning light I read the name on a sign, Oswiecem, a place unknown to me.

A few minutes later the train started to roll again. It was not a long ride. From far away I saw a series of buildings and as the train got nearer, I could see that the structures were barracks surrounded by barbed wire. Observation towers encircled the entire area.

The train then stopped in front of a wooden platform. Suddenly, the SS opened the boxcars and violently ejected us out of the cars onto the platform. There was no time to think; we had to move fast.

As I emerged from my boxcar I looked around in disbelief. From both sides of the railway tracks there was green grass, manicured so nicely, framed by colorful flowers. A group of inmates in striped clothes sat near where I stood, playing beautiful classical music. I could not comprehend the bizarre amalgamation of the inhuman conditions on the train, the screaming of SS troops, with the bucolic setting and enchanting music floating in the air. I felt a sense of relief, unaware of the suffering I would soon be forced to endure.

The men in striped clothes then moved quietly around us. Some children started to cry when the soldiers, trying to calm them, told them not to be afraid. This was the tactic used by the murderers to induce the victims to move like sheep to their final destination: the gas chambers.

We were placed in lines and ordered to move forward. Then we were approached by a group of military men led by a very handsome SS man dressed in a grey coat. I later learned that this was Dr. Mengele, the master of our destiny, the "Angel of Death." Waving with his hand, not talking, he decided the fates of the old, the sick, men, women and children.

The SS separated the healthy from the sickly, ordering the two groups to move in different directions. My group was directed toward the barracks. Women in stripes—the *Kapos* and their helpers—accompanied the SS men guarding us. They instructed us to disrobe and to separate our clothes from jewelry and other valuables. Unconsciously, I quickly grabbed a little earring from the little bundle of jewelry Fishel had given me and pushed it deeply into the lining of my shoe. This was my mother's earring, the only thing I carried with me into this place of death. Something inside had forced me to save this little treasure, which became my one source of hope. When I touched it I saw the beautiful image of my mother's face; the earring seemed to enjoin me not to give in to despair.

The SS warned us that the price for keeping any valuables was death. Regardless of the danger, I kept the earring throughout the war. Many years later, when my daughters married, each one received a gift from me.

Chapter 10 / Auschwitz

It was a little diamond ring, with a tiny stone from my mother's earring. Each ring had a blessing that they would never experience such horrors as their mother had.

By stripping the victims of their clothes and searching women's bodies for hidden jewelry, the beasts destroyed any remnant of dignity remaining to us. Naked, with shaking hands covering my breasts, I waited in line, not knowing what to expect. It was devastating for me to stand undressed among men and women, standing in line, to be tattooed. This was the moment when I became no more a human, when I was changed to a number—A-24490—a moment I can never forget. Even today, looking at the tattoo on my left arm, I can still feel the needle on my skin engraving my number. No more someone with a name, I was now A-24490, a small component in a destructive machine.

I felt so humiliated; helpless. But the dehumanizing process had not yet ended. We were forced into chairs where barbers cut our hair to the bare skin. In one moment we were changed into something unrecognizable. The roller coaster of destruction turned us scared souls into monsters.

I was one of the lucky few who were allowed to keep her hair, although I do not know why I was spared that humiliation. We were then forced to run in the nude to the *Bekleidungsamt* (clothing) building. Through the window clothes were distributed to us, regardless of size. Short women got a large size and tall ones got a short size. Quickly we began to exchange one with another, trying our best to find the right size to fit. Still looking grotesque, we had to move on. We were then led to our barracks, our place to live, to suffer and to die. There were three tiers of wooden planks upon which we were supposed to sleep. These bunks resembled a chicken house. I and a group of women from our city were ordered to take our places on the upper bunks.

I tried my best not to give into despair. Amid the torment I recognized Henia Maliniak, Gucia Stern, and her sister, Henia, who called out to me. Sobbing, we embraced each other and vowed, "Let us stay together and try to help each other not lose ourselves." It made me feel just a little better. But the approaching night filled me with dread.

Tired and shaking from cold and hunger, I could hardly move. I couldn't make peace with myself, having experienced so many indecencies in such a short time. Once a proud people, my friends and I, dressed in rags, our heads shaven, no longer looked like women.

With every passing minute it became darker and darker. A small bulb hung high in the middle of the barracks, spreading dull light—a gloomy dust over our heads turning us into silhouettes hard to recognize. I tried to gain some warmth by pressing my exhausted body close to my friends. But even moving from one side to the other, I felt the cold starting to penetrate my fatigued and weakened system.

My belly started to make noises from hunger, and an increasing pain inside my wrecked soul made me feel awful. Biting my lips, I cried silently.

Aching, I could not sleep. I needed to urinate. I whispered to Gucia, sleeping next to me, for help. In the darkness, holding hands, we slowly slid down in front of our sleeping bunk. Impossible to see, we bumped into moving shadows looking for a toilet. We followed the direction of a terrible odor in the air and found a moving line. Pushing slowly, one after the other, I came close and listened to the noise of the urinating shadows. Patiently waiting for my turn, I stretched out my hands and felt a bucket in front of me. This was the only way I could relieve myself. It was an awful feeling, but this was my world now. The misery I felt was indescribable.

We almost got lost on our return, but luckily I remembered the dull light in front of our bunk and retraced our steps in that direction. Exhausted, we climbed back up onto our bunk. It took a lot of energy, but we finally made it to our little spot. I dropped my helpless body onto the wooden board. Turning from one side to the other, closing my eyes, I forced myself to go to sleep, for how long a time I could not tell. Soon I was awakened by the noise around me and I was reminded of the hell in which I now lived.

Then began my first morning in Auschwitz. We were forced to run outside, five in a line, for the counting. I was so rundown from the night before, but I had to stand for hours, not moving till the counting was over.

Then, forced by the *Kapos*, I ran to get my first ration. Again, we had to stand in line, hungry, shaking from the cold. It took more than one hour but finally I got my ration, a tasteless mixture that had the texture of glue. We were also given a cup of a warm, dark solution that was supposed to be coffee. After ingesting this pitiful meal, I found a series of openings in the ground, the so-called toilets from which exuded a terrible stink from urine and excrement. As quickly as possible, one after another, we relieved ourselves. Then, we got back in the line, ready to go to work.

Like robots, we followed orders. My job was to move stones with my bare hands from one side of the fence to the other. After a few hours I could not move my fingers. My back ached from bending down so often to pick up the stones.

It was still hot under the August sun. My dress was wet with perspiration and stuck to my body. From all sides the SS forced us to toil, hitting the slow-moving inmates. Their anguish was so painful to witness. Afraid of

Chapter 10 / Auschwitz

being hit, I pushed my sore and tired body to lift yet another rock. This was only my first day; I could not see how I could take it much longer.

Finally there was a whistle, and we stopped working. Back into the line, supporting one another, we pushed our bodies to get our first so-called dinner, a dollop of watery soup mixed with half-cooked little pieces of rotten potatoes. I cried gazing at this meager portion that was supposed to be my source of sustenance. I looked around and saw ravished inmates using their fingers to consume every remnant of the vile-tasting food. We hardly felt human any longer.

I stared at my friends who had been staring at me. Closing my eyes, I raised my spoon and tried to swallow the awful smelling mixture. It stuck in my throat, making it almost impossible to swallow. Summoning all the strength remaining in my weary body, I forced it down. With shaking hands, I brushed the tears from my face and ate, trying not to think. It was so degrading. We were then made to hurry outside to wash our faces and hair in a line of sinks. Provided with bits of soap that contained hard little scraps that scratched our skin, we washed, and with nothing else to drink, drank the awful smelling water as well. With no time to wipe our faces, we were then forced to run back to our barracks.

Our misery was without end. Everywhere I was reminded of my subjugation—even in the air I inhaled and tasted. The sky, covered with a gray-brown cloud rising above into the horizon, was darkened from the smoke of human flesh burning in the crematoria. Day and night, without interruption, the killing machines poured tons of ash into the air. The smoke was terrible, getting into my nose so that I could hardly breathe. The ash left a bitter taste in my mouth.

We, the condemned, went on day in and day out, suffering. It seemed as if we were always running, constantly made to obey commands. I was part of a system organized and directed by the so-called Super Race, German Nazis who intended to devour human souls. I tried to resist the conditions to which I was subjected, especially the filth. One thing I was grateful for was that, because of malnutrition, I had stopped menstruating. I considered this a blessing, since there were no facilities to wash our dirty bodies.

The brutal behavior of the *Kapos* was a constant reminder of how helpless we were. When inmates fell out of line, the *Kapos* kicked them with their heavy boots. The weak and the sick could not take the bludgeoning, calling out for help as they were pummeled. I cried deeply in my soul, feeling the pain with every blow that hit the prostrate inmates. I was constantly afraid, not knowing what would happen next. I saw so many taken away, disappearing without a trace. What happened to those who did not return? In time, I found out that the sick were gassed and burned in the ovens of the crematoria in our camp. I constantly wondered when would my time come?

Whenever I felt most despondent and desperate, my Guardian Angel seemed to remind me that all was not lost. One morning, I was running along a fence when an unexpected voice called out "Chaiale" (Helen). Turning my head, I could not believe my eyes. My cousin, Shulim, who had been arrested by the Gestapo in 1940, was on the other side of the fence with a group of children. How incredible, I thought, that in this horrid place I had found my cousin. I remembered that on some Saturdays I would go with Fishel to my aunt's house where Shulim would read stories to me. Those had been happy moments in my life, when I was still free and beginning to open my eyes, listening and learning. But this happiness was taken from me. In planet Auschwitz there was no place for children; they grew old so quickly and died so young.

The next morning, while running for my ration, Shulim was again standing by the fence, looking for me. When I saw him, he motioned to me and threw a half loaf of bread through the opening in the fence. I had no idea of how he was able to get such a prized commodity, but I was too hungry to ask questions. I quickly grabbed the bread and put it inside my dress, under my arm. Back at the barracks, I shared the seeming gift from heaven with my friends. But that was the last time I saw Shulim. Wherever he is, may the Lord take care of him.

Hunger can turn a human into an animal. I had such a moment during my second month in Auschwitz. One evening, I stood in line for more that an hour to get my ration. Hungry and tired, I was the last in line. Finally I reached the pot to get my so-called soup. After scooping out my portion, the *stübedienst* (section servant) moved away. Seeing some soup still left, I was so hungry I could not resist reaching inside to devour the remaining portion. Suddenly I felt a hand grab me and rip out a handful of hair from my head. I was thrown to the ground and someone started to kick me and hit me with a big leather strap. Crying from the pain, I lay on the ground unable to move. Afterwards, Gucia came over with her sister and helped me get up.

One month passed. Then, in September, it rained days and days without interruption, and with every passing day it got colder and colder. Or clothes were constantly wet from the rain and stuck to our bodies, making it hard to move. Some of the inmates started to get sick. Lying on the wooden

Chapter 10 / Auschwitz

bunks in wet clothes made me feel so awful. I could not change my condition, but I dared not give up. I tried to convince myself that the Almighty was watching over me.

Always hungry, cold, pushing my tired body, I went on, not giving in. As the days became shorter and colder, the nights grew longer. Locked in a cage, the only road to escape was through the crematorium. That was the end. Death. Yet some of us found moments to forget our doomed lives and were able to build friendships with our fellow inmates. That feeling of belonging, of caring and of helping someone made me still feel human. But there were those who lacked compassion for others and often lost the will to fight, the will to survive. They were called *Musselman*, those who gave up, emotionless robots just waiting to end up in the ovens. But having with me a few friends from Radom, I did not feel lost.

I was particularly close to Gucia Maliniak and her sister, Henia. At nights, when it was impossible to sleep, the one thing that kept us alert was our determination not to give in to despair. We shared and recalled moments from our pasts, which make me feel good. I learned that Henia, so beautiful and so gentle, was the girlfriend of my brother, Morris. Now, here in this living hell, finding me gave her hope and energized her to go on. I looked after Henia, never letting her out of my sight. Whenever I got something, whether food or clothing, I always saved some for her.

Once, early in the morning, the *Kapos* came into our barracks to draft some women to clean the sidewalks in the camp. Outside it was raining and cold. To avoid being caught, we ran out into the open to the back of the barracks, trying to find a hiding place. Henia, running behind me, twisted her ankle and could not move. Gucia and I picked her up and pulled her along. I don't know where I found the strength, I only knew my friend was in pain and needed help. Everyday thereafter, we carried Henia to the *Appel* by forming a little seat with our hands and supporting her to enable her to stand during the counting. It was not easy for us, but it was the only way to help her.

Hunger put its mark on me. Sometimes I felt dizzy, walking unsteadily, but I tried with every strength left in my withering body to hold on. Living in such a hell left me in a relentless battle to survive. Like Sisyphus, I tried again and again, pushing my body against the rolling ball. My will forced my exhausted and weakened body to meet the challenge. With a fire burning in my mind, shaking, biting my lips, I tried to go on into the unknown. This was the way I was brought up, not to give in to despair and to try to face any hardship on my road. But some of us could not take the inhuman conditions.

Some women gave away their bodies for a cup of soup. My upbringing, especially my moral code, did not allow me to cross that line. My health was damaged, but I came out of the abyss morally unscathed. The most important thing for me was my strong belief in the Almighty.

One Sunday morning, running to get my ration, I saw an inmate on the other side of the fence calling to me in Polish, "*To dia ciebie*" ("This is for you"). He then produced a full pot of hot soup and, with a stick, he pushed the pot through the fence. I didn't know what to think, but my stomach told me to take the offering and to ask no questions. I grabbed the pot and ran as fast as I could back to the barracks. I shared the soup with Gucia and Henia. It was delicious. Each day thereafter the same man was waiting for me, and each day he pushed a pot of hot soup through the fence. I couldn't understand why someone I didn't know was trying to help me. Who was he? Looking through the wire I saw only a man in a striped coat smiling and staring at me.

At night, lying on the cold wooden bunk, wearing only a light dress and no underwear, the cold would slowly creep into my tired body, cutting deep into my heart. Unable to sleep, I lay there, shivering with chattering teeth. Just then, a thought occurred to me: Why not ask the stranger with the soup to get some clothes for me? I hesitated. Maybe he would be angry with me and I would lose the soup he had been providing. It was an inner fight in my soul, but after a long, sleepless night, I decided to try. The morning came and I shared my decision with Gucia, who cautioned me, "Be careful. Watch yourself."

Running close to the fence, as always, the man saw me and pushed another pot of soup toward me with a stick. Racing for the food, I asked him if it would be possible for him to get me a warm coat and a shirt. It was so cold and I was freezing. He looked at me, smiled, and said in Polish, "*Jutro dostaniesz*" ("Tomorrow I will bring them"). The words rang in my ears. I quickly grabbed the container of soup and ran away.

The next morning the man was waiting with a bundle under his arm. Seeing me come closer, he pushed the package along with the pot of soup through the wires. Nervously, I snatched the package and soup quickly, turned away and ran. It was a miracle. I felt the clothes through the wrapping of the package. I asked Gucia and her sister to stand around me while I pretended to clean my shoes. In seconds I took off my dress. Over my head the shirt came down, and then my coat was on. I could not believe how fast I had done it. I felt the clothes. They felt so good.

After so many cold nights, at last I felt a little warmer, but I still couldn't sleep. Always there was the noise and the crying of the inmates calling for help. The next morning came. My routine was to run along the fence, and as usual, the man was waiting. Again he pushed the little container with a stick, but when I reached out to grab it he smiled and said, "I would like to come over and to spend an evening with you." He told me he worked at the maintenance brigade and was free to move around the camp. It was a shock to me. Shaking, I forgot the soup and just ran away. His voice was loud, hollering after me, "I will see you in the evening."

Afraid, sweating all over my body, I found my friends and collapsed on the ground. My benefactor was not my friend—I would have to pay a price with my body for the things I had gotten from him. The price was too high for me. I could not think clearly. Gucia came over, embraced me, and tried to find out what had happened. "Helen, you were lucky. He could have hit you and harmed you," she said.

My struggle to survive was a fight without an end. I saw how some women in our barracks had been getting food, paying with their bodies. This was all they had to give away to end their hunger, but I could not do this. This was a line I could not cross. That night I lay in bed panicked by the possibility that the stranger might come looking for me. I had nowhere to escape. I sat up and hit my head on the bunk above. Then Gucia turned to me and said: "Chaiale, my sister and I will sit in front of the bunk. You lay down behind us. Just don't move. In this dull light nobody will find you." Quaking with fear, I lay down and prayed to the Almighty for help.

Later I could hear the voices of people moving around below, mixed with the crying of the sick. Then I heard the voice of a man and was petrified. My mind flooded with horrible thoughts of this man forcing himself on me, demanding that I give in to him. I could not have gone on living with such humiliation. In the morning Gucia told me that there was a man, an inmate in a striped coat, walking around looking for me. He had been searching for maybe an hour before he finally left. Never again would I run close to that fence, and never again would I receive the bonus of soup.

September turned into October, and the rains continued. It poured day and night and our conditions grew worse and worse. The most painful time was early in the morning at the *Appel*, shivering for hours in soaked clothing. Some of us could not take it, falling into the mud wherever they stood, crying pathetically for help. I stood, shaking, and thinking about who was better off, the ones who would not suffer any more or those of us still alive, going on in pain and slowly dying?

We went on suffering; so many died every day. For me, there were no more tears; they had dried out in my soul. We got used to the dying voices.

We also got used to the beatings by the SS. But I could not understand how we, so weak and starving, could go on.

PART III
FREEDOM

CHAPTER ELEVEN
OBERALTSTADT

I was in Auschwitz for only four months, but it seemed like a lifetime. Then one morning, in November 1944, *Kapos* entered our barracks and ordered us to form a long line in front of our sleeping quarters. I was in the first line, standing in the mud, shaking from the cold, not knowing what would be next. An icy wind swept over us, and it started to rain. We stood in wet clothes, shivering, holding on to each other, not moving, surrounded by the SS.

I was afraid that this was the selection time, that some of us might be directed toward the gas while others would be sent to the hospital to be used for medical experiments. Previously, even healthy, strong women had been sent to the hospital from which they never returned. I had such a terrible feeling, fearing that maybe I was the next one to go.

Then I saw a group of men in civilian clothes walking with the SS in our direction. Coming close in front of the line, the men started to select some women. I was ordered to move out from the line to one side. In a distance, about twenty yards away, some one hundred women were selected to form another line. The others went back to the barracks. It was quiet. I stood there frozen, shivering from the cold, waiting.

Gucia and Henia Stern and Henia Maliniak were in line with me. Then I saw that two other women from Radom, Thema Cukier and Gina Rychtam, were in the same group. The SS ordered us to move out. We were told we were going to the bathhouse, but I was petrified, because I knew that some bathhouses were actually gas chambers. After we stepped into the bathhouse, we were ordered to take off our clothes. We could only take our shoes with us. Before entering the shower room we were ordered to place our shoes on the side so we could have them when we came out. Then we were given pieces of soap and forced into a large chamber. I feared that at any moment poisonous gas would envelope us and end our miserable existence. But inside the room a miracle happened: water began to gush over us. We were actually taking a shower! I had forgotten how long it had been since I could wash my itching body. It felt so good.

Then we toweled off our wet bodies. Naked, with only shoes in hand, they forced us to run outside to the *Bekleidungs* building. There we got clothes which had previously belonged to the condemned souls who had been forced into the *Himmel Komando* (crematorium). The clothes were in good condition, having been washed and made ready to be sent to Germany for the *Winter Hilf* (winter aid) groups to wear.

(A Jew had no value to the killers when he or she was alive, but after the victims were slaughtered and their carcasses burned, every bit of what was left over was used. Women's hair was used to make clothes for U-boat men or for mattresses; gold from teeth was used to buy military materials for the SS killing machine; ashes were used for fertilizer. The value of a dead Jew had been set at a price of twenty Reichsmarks.)

I could not understand what was going on. Afraid that someone would take them away, I quickly dressed in the clothes I was given. A civilian group entered the room to inspect us. They told us not to be afraid, that we were leaving Auschwitz for the Siemens Motor plant in Oberaltstadt, located in northern Czechoslovakia. They would take care of us as long as we followed orders. At last we knew where we were going. It was a relief, just thinking that I would be away from the crematoria. It could not be worse than here, where the smoke and stench from burning human flesh was a constant reminder of what awaited us. From a commodity destined for the ovens, I had been tranformed into a slave, working for Siemens Industries.

That night we were assigned to different sleeping facilities, with wooden bunks with blankets. It was warm and clean inside.

Early in the morning, after breakfast, we were marched to the railroad station located just outside the camp. There we were loaded into a cattle train destined for our new working place. Sitting on the floor, the cold wind blew in through an opening and penetrated our clothes. I felt so cold. I moved closer to my friends, trying to protect myself from the frigid wind. This helped a little bit. An SS man in every boxcar watched us, making sure we could not move.

Chapter 11 / Oberaltstadt

A whole day passed, sitting, leaning one on the other. My shivering body moved to the rhythm of the rolling train, back and forth. With half-opened eyes I tried to sleep. Henia Stern was close by, pressing my hand and quietly whispering. "Hold me, Chaiale, I feel so sick." Tears were running down her beautiful face. She started to vomit. Gucia and I tried to help her, cleaning her clothes with a wet piece of material. She was slowly getting weaker and weaker; it was horrifying to look at her. We had some water, but she needed medication.

As the train rambled on I sat and looked at her. What could I do to help? She held on tightly to my hand and with wandering eyes called in a hoarse voice, "Morris, where are you? I need you. Please don't let me die. I love you so much."

Listening to her, I felt devastated, knowing I couldn't help. I was overwrought, wondering what I could do to ease her suffering. Gucia and I tried whatever was possible to help her, to no avail. It was torture for me. The situation grew more hopeless as she became weaker with every passing hour. I felt myself getting sick, being so close to Henia, powerless to ease her pain.

The train rolled on and on, the noise of the moving wheels cut deeply into my head. At the start of our journey I hadn't sensed it, but after a few hours I felt as if my head was being battered. Holding my hands to my ears, I passed out. I came to when the train violently stopped. The jolt was so strong that we all fell on top of one another inside the car. Henia was holding on to me crying loudly, "Help me. I can't take any more." Others around us were pushed into one another.

When we stood up the SS men slid open the doors and screamed at us, "*Raus! Macht schnell!*" ("Get out! Move fast!"). They hit the people in front of us so they would move faster. I grabbed Henia, lifting her with the help of her sister, and pushed through the mass of people and into the open. The first moment the fresh air hit our faces I felt revived. We were at a small railroad station, surrounded by mountains off in the horizon. Nearby were some houses and trees covered with snow. It was winter in Oberaltstadt, our destination.

Given no time to rest, we were forced to walk about twenty minutes, pulling Henia along the way. We arrived in front of a complex of buildings. The civilians who had selected us in Auschwitz took charge, telling us not to worry. They informed us that from now on we would be working for the Siemens Motors plant in Oberaltstadt. This was where we would live and work. Just obey orders and work, they instructed, and they would take care of us.

We entered a building, dragging Henia with us. We stepped into a large, heated room, with wooden beds covered with blankets. An oven stood in the middle of our new quarters. We took three beds close to each other, with Henia between Gucia and myself. Immediately we started to take care of Henia, taking her clothes off, putting her on the bed, and washing her with lukewarm water. She was on fire. The door was locked from the outside so there was no one to ask for help. After a while the civilians brought a big kettle with soup and some bread cut into pieces. We all received utensils consisting of a cup, a little pot, and a spoon. It was a comfort that we would no longer have to stand outside to get our rations. Gucia went and brought the ration for me, herself and her sister, but Henia couldn't eat. Delirious, she moaned, "I am dying. A fire is burning in my body. I cannot breathe."

Quickly we took some towels, wetted them, and washed her body. It helped, but after a short while she couldn't take any more. The fever was taking over her mind and body. She started jumping up and down on her bed and white mucus formed around her mouth. Staring at me, she shrieked in a loud and hoarse voice, "Morris, where are you? I need you. Please help me. Don't let me die. I love you so much." She started ripping hair from her head and screamed, "I am dying."

Tears covered her beautiful young face. She beat her chest with her fists—her soul was leaving her tired and sick body to meet her Creator. Sitting close to her, I was frozen, part of me dying looking at her trying to hold on, not to give in. It was so devastating for me. She was so young and beautiful, in the bloom of her life, yet she was dying. Silently, raising my eyes to the sky, I whispered the prayer for those about to die, "*Sh'ma Yisroel, Adonai Elohaynu, Adonai Echod!*" ("Blessed be the name of His glorious kingdom for ever and ever!").

I sat for hours looking at Henia, sobbing, staring at her face. At least she was not suffering any more. May her soul rest in peace. Gucia wailed, "Chaiale, she is gone. My sister is dead. Now I am alone. It is so painful for me. I don't know why she died. She had everything to live for. I am older; Henia gave me some things to live for. Now she is dead. I haven't anyone to care for. She was the last of our family alive after the slaughter." She ripped at her hair, hitting her fists on her chest, calling aloud, "Why *Gotenyu* (God) did she have to die? Why not me?"

I tried to comfort her, embracing her. It touched me so deeply. I had never been so close to someone who had just died. I didn't have the words to cheer up Gucia. What could I say? I was too heartbroken,

Chapter 11 / Oberaltstadt

shocked and disheartened. Together, holding hands, we did not take our eyes from Henia's body.

After many hours, our guards opened the doors. We had to carry the body outside. Gucia bent over Henia's body, kissed her forehead, and in a loud, lamentable voice cried, "My dear Henia. Why you? Better I should die. You left me in the hands of these murderers. I am alone now in pain. I love you. May you rest in peace, my dear sister."

I pulled her away. The SS were now standing around ordering us to get ready for work.

This was our first morning in Oberaltstadt, and it was so sad. In a hurry we got our cup of coffee and a piece of bread and were on our way to our working place. Walking on the road covered with snow, I saw the sky above was slowly getting lighter and lighter. I looked at the clear horizon—no more smoke, no crematoria.

We seemed to be walking through a forest, with bent branches frosted with snow and ice. And for the first time in recent memory, I breathed deeply and felt the fresh air penetrating into my heart. Despite the presence of SS men and some women in military uniforms with dogs on leashes who escorted us, the surroundings were so beautiful.

When we reached the village it was still early in the morning, so there were no people on the streets. Then we approached buildings that looked like airplane hangars with sliding metal doors. This is where we would work. Stopping in front, the SS men handed papers to a civilian, our German supervisor, who signed them. He explained that from now on we would be working for Siemens Motor Works, making parts for airplane engines. We were told not to be afraid, that in a short time we would learn how to operate machinery that would produce things for the German Army. He then led a group of us to some drilling machines which he proceeded to teach us to operate.

I took my time, but I learned. The supervisor came by and inspected, making some corrections. He didn't holler in the shrill, rasping voice to which I had become so accustomed. Instead, he calmly explained to me my mistakes. He told me not to worry, that within a few days I would learn everything about the machine. Never before had I been spoken to so gently in German. His approach and tone was so different from that of the brutal SS that it left me breathing much easier.

In the evening, when we returned to our quarters, no longer was someone standing behind us, ordering our every movement.

We soon discovered that we were not the only slaves working in this place—some young Italian men were among us, working, singing and smiling.

The working conditions were so different from the warehouse outside Auschwitz. Here was a separate toilet for men and women and a wash place to clean our hands. Assisting our supervisor was a group of German women, instructing us on how to do the work. Some of them were very nice, leaving pieces of bread and apple from their lunch. At first we were afraid to touch these items for fear of being punished, and so the food lay in front of us for hours. But at quitting time some of us couldn't resist. We grabbed the leftovers and ran away with them. Still, the two rations we received each day weren't enough to meet the harsh conditions. Also, our light clothes were insufficient for the freezing temperatures; some of us got sick and had to stay in the barracks. They stayed confined with no medicine or help, but unlike at Auschwitz, they were not taken away to be shot. Some died in their beds and were then buried behind the barracks, just covered with frozen soil. Those who recovered, returned to work.

I could not forget any of them, my heart still cries for those who had died so young. Sometimes in the morning I would stand in front of the graves and recite prayers. What a waste of lives, I lamented. So many cut off before their time; so many dreams that would not be fulfilled.

A few months later spring was in the air. Grass began to grow, flowers emerged and birds took flight. Everywhere there were signs of new beginnings—except for us whose fate it was to go on suffering. Despite the changes taking place about us, there were no changes in our schedule, which required us to work from morning until evening at the drilling machines. Time didn't stop. Through the windows I could see the trees coming back to life, but for my friends and me coming back to life was possible only in dreams.

At night I closed my eyes and I was back in time at the meadow with Fishel, running around, picking up white and yellow daisies. I was calling my brother, "Fishel," when Henia Maliniak shook me awake. "I had such a beautiful dream," I told her. "I was walking in the meadows with Fishel, picking up flowers. I was so happy. It is so hard to look and see the changes around us—deprived of enjoying the beauty of the changes in nature. It makes me feel so sad. Are we different from the others? Why do we have to suffer?" Henia just looked at me, staring.

My body began revolting from the shortage of food. It was particularly painful to work at midday, looking at the German women enjoying their lunches. It made me feel so hungry.

One week passed after another and we grew progressively weaker, the

Chapter 11 / Oberaltstadt

clothes hanging on our thin bodies. I pushed my tired body, often holding on to Henia, trying desperately to go on. My mind, still alert, offered me the only avenue of escape.

My sadness and mournfulness began to change into anger. I decided that I had to do something to get back at the Germans. So after the foreman inspected my work, I deliberately miscalibrated the grinding mechanism so as to damage the finished pieces before putting them into the wooden boxes that would be shipped to the army. Caught, I would be killed, but I continued to sabotage my work because it made me feel that I was somehow getting back at my oppressors.

In March 1945, I noticed changes in the behavior of the German women. They became more and more nervous, and constantly whispered to one another. Their smiles also disappeared from their faces.

Along with the spring rains came the sounds of high-flying airplanes that awakened us in the middle of the night. By the middle of April more changes occurred in our work place. A group of SS arrived and started to dismantle some machines, packing them in big wooden containers that were then taken away by large transport trucks. We watched and waited, aware that something was going on. We still received our rations, but they were reduced to just once a day. We continued to walk every morning to the plant, but instead of working we sat around and waited. Our supervisor came, looked around, and quietly left. I could see a change in his behavior as well. Before leaving, he went to his locker and, turning around to look at me, shook his head and whispered, "May the Lord take care of you." This was the last time I ever saw him.

The German women still showed up at the factory. Once, they asked for a few of us to go with them and help dig up potatoes. For a few hours we worked outside in the field and in the evening in our room Gucia and I peeled potatoes and mixed them with water. We added some little pieces of bread and cooked the mixture on the oven to make soup. It tasted good and we savored it, particularly since our rations had been getting smaller and smaller.

Toward the end of April the snow disappeared and grass began covering the sidewalks. From my window I could see little leaves slowly growing and covering their branches. Other changes were afoot as well. The SS were still around watching us, but the women and the dogs had disappeared. Also the thunder and lightning from the distant guns had grown increasingly louder. Frightened, not knowing what was going to happen to us, the SS men, too, appeared nervous as they walked around our quarters, watching us. It was so terrible to wait, not knowing what they would do to us.

CHAPTER TWELVE
MAY 1945

With my friends lying sick in their beds, starving and crying from the pain, afraid to move, I sat on the floor staring at the door, thinking that at any moment the SS would come in and end us all. Through the window I could see the Nazi guards walking with bottles of vodka in their hands, drinking and smoking cigarettes. We, on the other hand, lingered on the edge of extinction, starving, with only water to drink.

Spring is my favorite time of year, when nature awakens from its long winter sleep. The scenery outside took my breath away. From the window I could see the wide-open sky framed by mountains. Earlier, I had no time to appreciate the world outside our barracks, but now, confined in our quarters, I saw the beautiful surroundings. I marveled at the early morning sun slowly appearing on the horizon, spreading the first sparkle of light. Then, like a ball rolling out of its confines, the fully formed sun shot golden lines of light into the sky, piercing through little moving clouds and then disappearing. The imposing mountains were still covered with snow in some places, like little white pads. The setting was a work of art in which the painter added with a light touch of his brush some green shadows surrounding the white little dashes of snow. The rays from the shining sun, floating between the mountains, added a finishing touch to this unusually beautiful landscape. I never saw such beautiful scenery.

Lost in such reverie I almost forgot where I was, but only for a moment. While moving my head, I touched the cold glass of the window which instantly brought me back to my tragic reality. Tears welled up in me as I reveled in nature's beauty, which used to be my world but was no longer.

Here I was in the full bloom of youth, admiring the wonder and beauty of nature so close I could almost reach out and touch it. Yes, before me, through the window, was life and beauty, but I was in the confines of my barracks where my friends lay sick and starving, where I could feel the shadow of death floating in the air.

My body was weak and overcome by a horrible feeling of helplessness. I could hardly move. Saddened, I contemplated my destiny: I was born in the wrong place and time, and my spirit was slowly being crushed.

Moving away from the window, I heard Henia call: "Help me. I am so hungry." With no food available, I gave her a cup of water, hoping it would sustain her. As the days passed we became weaker and weaker, for some movement all but impossible.

On the night of May 7, I could not sleep at all. The hunger and the noises in my stomach made me feel dizzy and weak. I couldn't take any more. It was too much for me. Penetrating the darkness of the night was the thunder from the heavy guns and the streaks of light cutting across the horizon, one after the other. The ground shook from falling bombs. We sat in the dark room for hours, waiting and waiting, as the noises grew louder and louder, the bombs seemingly falling closer to where we were.

As the dawn broke we heard voices in Yiddish calling loudly, "*Die SS zenen verschwinden*" ("The SS have disappeared"). Still afraid, we did not move. Then came loud voices and a knocking on the door. A voice rang out, proclaiming: "We are free. No more Germans around." Still afraid, I could not believe it. A few minutes passed before I realized what had happened. It was a shock to me. Slowly, I moved my weary body to the window and looked down. I saw many of my friends running around, jumping. I opened the window and could hear laughter—the voices of so-called slaves, singing and dancing. Turning around, looking at my sick friends, I stared to cry, but this time I shed tears of joy. I felt overwhelmed and confused. What do I do now? What will become of us?

I collected myself and went outside to where they had buried Henia Stern. I stood there and thought how sad it was that she didn't live to enjoy this moment. Already in some places grass was growing around the few stones marking her grave. Shaking my head and patting the ground, I raised my eyes to the sky, pleading: "Lord, didn't we suffer enough. Please take care of her young soul. I am lost with nowhere to go. Please guide me. I don't know what to do."

I was a survivor—alive, but sick in body and soul. This was the moment I had hoped for, free from physical pain and no longer afraid. Yet I wasn't

Chapter 12 / May 1945

truly free. Where to go? What will I do? I am alone. I found it very difficult to accept the changes that had just taken place.

CHAPTER THIRTEEN
THE END OF SLAVERY

At first Russian soldiers entered our camp, but they were soon replaced by American GIs. Now we no longer had to scavenge for food. The American soldiers provided us with plenty to eat and I voraciously devoured anything I could get my hands on. I ate without end, but my system couldn't take it and I became sick, as was the case with so many others. Once the Americans realized that we could not handle unlimited quantities of food, they set up special kitchens that carefully doled out portions we could digest. Our liberators provided medical help for the sick as well, but many former prisoners died. Some perished because they were too sick; others got diarrhea from overeating. Some expired because they could not take the changes; it just became too much for them. Many of them were single survivors, the only members of their families to escape liquidation at the hands of the Nazis. Alone, feeble, and nowhere to go, they lost their will to live and soon after liberation died in their sick beds. It was so sad. So many died. There was so much suffering and starvation—living skeletons just waiting to die, despite their newfound freedom.

The Americans took good care of us, providing us with clothes and shoes. Most importantly for us women, we could wash. Sowly we started to look human again. But despite the welcome changes, we had difficulty adjusting to our new conditions. I spent sleepless nights wondering if and when I would see my family. How about my mother and father? How about my brothers? Did they survive? I cried and prayed to the Almighty for their safety. I clung to the hope that some of my family managed to survive the Nazi scourge. Maybe mother. Or maybe my father had survived.

They had been in the bloom of their lives. I couldn't think about my brothers. The last time I had seen them was on the way to Tomaszow. Just thinking of losing them made me feel terribly alone. Sometimes I would dream of Fishel. Oh, I loved him with all my heart.

At the age of twenty-three all I had were memories of my home and my family. I couldn't forget the last words Fishel had spoken to me in 1943 at the liquidation of the small ghetto in Radom: "Chaiale, I have vowed to our father that I will do everything possible to take care of you. I remember our father's last words. "Don't forget Chaiale. This is my only daughter. Take care of her." Whenever I could I would turn to the Almighty and ask Him to take care of Fishel. Only after that would I ask the Almighty to take care of me and give me the strength and the energy to face my painful destiny.

Now, at the moment when I was free, I could only think of getting to Radom to see Fishel. I was debilitated and in pain, but the hope of seeing my family gave me the will to overcome my sickness. I asked Henia if she would accompany me to Radom. She answered: "I will go with you. I, too, am looking for your brother Sam. I am alone. Maybe he survived. He is the only one for whom I have to look. My family, all of them, were sent to Treblinka in 1942 at the liquidation of the ghetto. Yes, I will go with you."

At the end of May 1945, Europe was in chaos. Roads were engorged with refugees from every country, some trying to leave, some returning and some wandering aimlessly. We Holocaust survivors presented unique problems which the occupation authorities were not prepared to deal with. They set up temporary facilities for survivors called displaced persons camps, or DP camps. Many survivors stayed in the camps while trying to decide where to go for permanent residence. Some left the camps, and with no other place to go, wandered from one country to another. Others tried to return to their places of birth, looking for members of their families who perhaps had withstood the Nazi slaughter. Survivors found it difficult to believe that the Nazis had murdered most of their kin, but the hope of reconnecting with loved ones kept them going.

When I was liberated, the Americans told us to go back to our hometowns. For some of us, home was Germany, the land of the exterminators. And many Germans still continued to regard survivors as racial inferiors who threatened their blood and their soil. Others took to the road to return to Poland, home to three million Jews before the war.

At the end of May 1945, the guns were silenced. Since there were no frontiers, it made it easy to move from one country to another, especially in those parts occupied by the victors. The occupying forces tried to help the

Chapter 13 / The End orf Slavery

survivors to get to their places of origin, but transportation presented a huge problem in Eastern Europe where railroads had been destroyed. Consequently, roads in all directions swarmed with refugees traveling on foot, by horse and by military vehicle.

I was liberated in northern Czechoslovakia, not on German soil, so I felt safe traveling about. The Czechs, having suffered tremendously at the hands of the Nazis, were very friendly to survivors, offering food and shelter. The route to Poland went through Prague, where international groups and American Jewish organizations fed and housed us. In this capital of the Czech Republic I met many Jewish people, survivors from Poland.

It took several days to get the appropriate papers before Henia and I were on our way to Radom. Again, I was filled with anxiety about my family, wondering whether any were still alive. I was afraid not knowing whom I would meet coming back to my house in Radom. I found comfort in thinking about my relatives. I hoped to see them. It had been so many years since I had seen my mother. What about my father? How about Fishel and my other brothers? It was torture for me, just thinking that some of them might have perished. I prayed to God to give me strength so that I could face the moment of meeting them.

The last hours before arriving at Radom were for me the most nerve-wracking; my heart beat so loudly. I was sweating. I felt so excited I could not wait. The moment the train pulled into Radom, I grabbed Henia by the hand and ran from the station toward the house where I grew up. I could not believe what I saw along the way: The streets had not changed; they were just as I remembered. I walked along Trauguta Street, then on to Zeromskiego Street. I could see houses from both sides of the street. All were the same as when I had left the city.

Tears rolled down my face as I approached the corner of Walowa Street, not far from my home. It looked to me just as it had always been. Coming to the corner of Walowa and Peretza, I had to stop and take a deep breath. I was only a few houses away from my home. Excited, I yelled, "Henia just a few more houses and I will be back with my family." I still believed that I would see all of them. Coming to my house at Peretza 3, I did not look, just ran up the steps. I knocked at the door, breathlessly waiting to see which one of my loved ones would open it. Someone inside responded; the noise of the turning key opening the door made me feel nervous. Shaking with anticipation, I got ready to greet someone from my family. What happened then I never will forget. A strange man opened the door, looked at me and scornfully uttered, "*Co ty szukasz Zyd?*" ("What are you looking for, Jew?"). Choking with tears, trembling, I could barely speak. Finally, I said, "My, my family used to live here." He slammed the door in front of me, hollering, "Never come back. The Germans killed your family. This is not your home anymore."

For seconds I was frozen at the entrance to the building. I was in shock; in an instant my dreams were completely shattered. This was the most devastating moment in my life. Still, I couldn't believe it. I looked at the door again and again to make sure I was in the right place. Yes, it was the apartment where my family and I had lived. Everything was the same. But this familiar place was suddenly now strange and hostile.

I couldn't take any more. I ran down the steps, crying. I couldn't talk. Henia embraced me. The only words that came out from both of us were, "What will we do?" We had to cry to let out our disappointment and bitterness. Where were we to go? Strangers passed us on the street, animated in conversation. Then, surprisingly, we heard some people speaking in Yiddish. Approaching them, we found out that some Jews were now living in the city. We went with them to the Pasternaks, people who had known my family. At last we had a place to stay. But I was still depressed and confused, feeling very much alone.

The desire to see my family had kept me alive; now, I didn't have any desire to go on. Everything was gone. I was a lost soul in a country that had become the graveyard of my family, my people. That night I could only sleep a few minutes—awakening, shaking. I couldn't make peace with my sad reality. The Pasternaks had been one of the few families to survive the carnage. Two brothers, a sister, a sister-in-law, Sonia Zlotnik, along with her brother and her two sisters emerged from the Holocaust to start a new life. I was so envious. There was not a single surviving member of my family, just me.

Through the window the moon was on the horizon, spreading its dull light. The blinking stars made me forget my grief for but a second. Sorrow, humiliation, and personal tragedy had followed me in my youth. I didn't have time to grow up. I had been exposed to a life of cruel and painful struggle at such a tender age. Now I was free once again, but I felt more grief than when I was in the hands of the murderers. At least in the camps I had hope that some day I would be reunited with my loved ones. Now, this too, was taken from me. Even in the barracks I could dream and think of better tomorrows; now, I didn't have one.

It was a long and painful night. In the morning Shewa Pasternak came into my room and said: "Chaiale, I know how hard it is for you. But remember,

Chapter 13 / The End orf Slavery

Sonia Zlotnik once was at Szkolna camp. There she told us that your aunt Frania Fink, your father's sister, was in Warszawa, where she stood as a beggar in front of a church. Why don't you go to where she lived in Zamosc? Do not give up. Maybe she is there." I looked at her, "Yes, I remember. You were there at the same barracks when Sonia came in and told you about her. But I forgot. Too many things have been on my mind. Now you have given me some hope."

While we there, other Jews came to the Pasternak's house. They, too, had been wandering from city to city looking for surviving members of their families. Shewa asked them where they came from. They recounted that two days ago, as they were passing through Zamosc, they stayed at the home of Frania Fink, the only Jew in town. Shewa shouted, "Chaiale, didn't I tell you to go there. Never lose hope. You aren't alone any more. *Your Aunt Frania is alive; go there."

Turning to Henia I said, "You, too, are coming with me. Wherever I go, you, too, are going." She didn't say a word, just nodded her head. Shewa packed a bundle with food for us and soon we were on the road to Zamosc. After traveling a few days by truck, by horse and by carriage, we reached the city. It took no time at all to find my aunt, since she was well known in Zamosc.

My aunt sat with me for hours sharing her anguish and painful life during the war. During the occupation my aunt had sold her hardware store to a Polish friend, with the understanding that in case some of the family survived he would sell it back to them after the war, which he did.

For more than thirty years our family had lived in this little town where gentiles lived in peace with their Jewish neighbors. Their children grew up together, played together, and attended the same schools. The only difference was their religion. Friday afternoons the Jews closed their enterprises in preparation for the Sabbath. The Christian Polish population observed Sundays for their religious practices. Sometimes there were little disturbances, but mostly the population continued to live and to conduct its business without any uneasiness.

That was the relationship before the Nazis occupied this area of Poland. Everything changed after September 1939, when the Nazis built a wall between the Polish and Jewish population. As I was listening I could not believe how this woman had overcome the hardships she had endured during the past six years. The story of her survival was no less incredible than mine.

CHAPTER FOURTEEN
MY BLEEDING HEART

At the time of liberation I was twenty-three years old. Physically I had recovered, but inside my heart was bleeding. I could not feel and enjoy the change. All during my captivity I had waited for the moment when I would be free. But when it actually came, it was a disappointment. The only desire I had was to see and join my family again and to begin a new life. This gave me the will and the power to survive. But now, knowing that most of my family had perished, I was alone in a strange world. I had nowhere to turn; I was lost. Yes, I had found my aunt, but I had lost the closest members of my family. My mother, my father, my brothers had been murdered in Nazi slaughter places. It was so hard for me to make peace with reality.

My Aunt did not know when she kissed me, said goodnight, and closed the door, that I started to cry. I so missed my loved ones, especially Fishel. He had put his life on the line to save me. Just the thought of seeing him again had kept me going. I hadn't had the time to say goodbye to him. Knowing that he was gone felt like a knife cutting deep into my heart. I felt so miserable.

Quietly sobbing, I tried to sleep but couldn't. How sad it was for me to think that everything was lost. I tried to find something which would lift my spirits and restore my will to go on. Then I remembered my father's words, "Believe in our Creator. He will never let you down. Remember, for thousands of years we have lived in despair, and we survived. Only with His guidance can we face the hostile world. I hope and pray to the Almighty. Only with His help can we overcome this so violent time."

The next morning I went for a walk to a nearby park. I sat on a bench and looked at the trees and the flowers. They were so beautiful. It was summer in Poland. Birds were flying around and butterflies of so many beautiful colors were in the air. Nature, after a long winter, was alive. Raising my eyes to the sky, I saw no clouds to mar the perfect blue heaven. The rising sun shone on the horizon, painting my surroundings with a yellow streak. The light hit the still wet flowers and turned them into gold, while the drops fell to the ground like little golden pearls.

I had always been enthralled by nature's majesty, yet in my heart I could feel no joy. I could not revel in the beautiful scenery; I could only think of my irreplaceable loss. My soul was full of pain. My mind could not think right. My dreams were gone. I needed time to make peace with my sad reality and to look for something that would awaken in me the will to go on, to face my destiny.

My Aunt Frania became my savior, my guiding light. She was the one who restored my lost desire to fight and not give in to despair. She spent every Sunday with me, talking for hours and hours. With time, I became closer to her. Like my mother, she tried to build up in me the belief not to give up.

"Chaiale, I am older than you." she said, "The best years of my life are behind me. After so much suffering, I am not alone. I found you. You are young. You still have a future to look forward to. I have money and a business. You are to me a daughter. Do not worry. I will take care of you. Everything that I own will be yours some day. Who else do I have? Together, we cannot give in. You have to try not to lose hope. You never know, maybe your brothers are still alive. Please do not give up hope. Just believe in the Almighty. He will not let you down."

Day after day she talked to me, trying to reassure me that there was a tomorrow. I began to feel better; I, too, started to believe maybe some of my brothers had survived. I tried not to lose hope, thinking about them. I started to dream again. I had overcome indescribable hardships and I would not allow my personal tragedies to defeat me. I told Henia, "Let us not lose hope. We never know for sure. We can't give in to despair. Maybe Sam and Fishel have survived. Let's hope."

One morning, while helping my aunt at the store, some Jewish people came in asking for Frania. The visitors spoke to her in Yiddish and gave her a letter written by her daughter. My Aunt started crying and said loudly, "Chaiale, my daughter is alive. I told you, do not lose hope. Remember, don't ever give up, and believe. However long it takes, the Almighty will

Chapter 14 / My Bleeding Heart

help you. Remember this." This fortified me and made me believe that miracles were still possible.

And a miracle did indeed happen. It was at the end of June, as I was helping out at my Aunt's store, on a day I will never forget. I was looking at the door and suddenly my brother Morris appeared. He entered the store crying out, "Chaiale. Finally, I have found you."

It was a shock to me. Here he was, my brother, Morris, in front of me. Frozen for the moment, I just stared at him. I started to cry, hugging him and calling, "Morris, Morris, I love you and I was missing you so much." I was so overwhelmed. It took me a while before I cried out to our aunt. "Aunt Franis, my brother Morris is here! I can't believe it!" She came running and turned to me and said, "Didn't I tell you never to give up hope? Now you aren't alone."

Then, turning to Morris, I asked. "Where is Fishel?" Morris did not like to bring me the sad news. "First of all, four of us survived." I was waiting to hear from him the names of my surviving brothers. "Herman, Sam, Jacob, they survived." I quickly interrupted. "How about Fishel?" Morris lowered his eyes and softly said, "He did not survive. He was killed in Dachau, a few hours before the Americans liberated us."

I thought I would die. I passed out, falling to the ground. I could not think. I was lost. I didn't know where I was. My whole world fell apart. The most important person in my life, the one for whom I was looking and hoping to see, was dead. Gone forever. Closing my eyes I called, "Lord didn't you punish me enough? Why did you take Fishel away from me?" I was in such pain. Ripping my hair, hitting my fists on my chest, I shook my head back and forth, sobbing. My brother and my aunt lifted me from the floor, trying to comfort me. I constantly asked, "Why did he have to die? He was so strong. I would give my life to bring him back."

Morris and Henia did what they could to soothe my pain. Both of them reminded me, "Remember, you aren't alone. Four of your brothers have survived. From now on we will be together. We will take care of you. Remember you are young. Nothing can happen to us now. We lived through the Nazi hell and now we are alive. Together we will try to build our future." But their voices could not reach me. I could not think. I was so mixed up.

For hours and hours I lay on my bed crying. Henia brought me some food. Pushing away the tray and lying down on the bed, I tried to sleep. I felt so lonely. It was so difficult for me. The dream of seeing Fishel had kept me going. Now he was gone, lost forever.

I couldn't comprehend how I could face such a heartbreaking loss. I tried to pray to God, asking Him not to leave me and to help me in this moment of sorrow. Then a voice inside of me tried to reason with my soul. "You aren't alone anymore. Four of your brothers survived the hell. Let go and be together with them. You were alone so long. Remember, they are your brothers."

A few days later, I awakened early in the morning while everyone else was asleep. I went to the garden, sat on the bench and looked around. The sun was slowly appearing on the horizon like a conductor with his baton slowly moving. The rays started to penetrate the branches that under their gentle touch had been slowly moving, turning the yellow color into a golden light shadow. It was like an orchestra following the movements of the baton of their maestro as they started to move from one branch to another—slowly, then increasing their speed. To me it was like a beautiful sound from an orchestra, playing a sweet symphony of nature awakening from a short summer nap to life. Like a ballerina with her toes gently touching the floor, so the rays moved from one branch to the other, without interruption, increasing their movements, then disappearing.

The movement of birds filled the air. Their noise, so low, disturbed the morning silence, adding a final touch to the majestic setting. For me it was like a sound of flutes joining together to play a beautiful melody in honor of our Lord, thanking Him for this masterpiece of His own creation. This masterpiece in living color was so beautiful. I felt so good.

Nature did not change; I had changed. The long years of suffering and humiliation still could not destroy the feeling of beauty in my soul. The pain and suffering had made me a better human being. The murderers had not been able to take away my dreams and aspirations. Breathing the fresh air so deep inside, I felt alive again. Rising my head to the sky, I whispered, praying to the Creator, "Lord, thank you for taking care of me. At last I am not alone any more. Thank you for giving me back my brothers. Please guide me so that I can meet my destiny. My life is in Your hands. So far, You have watched over me. You are the One who gave me the strength to overcome the forces of evil."

I went back to the house, saying to myself, "Chaiale, you have to be strong. A new challenge is in front of you. You can do it. Never give up. Life is not a paradise. You always have to be alert and never lose faith."

That night I was able to sleep deeply. I felt relieved that the worst was behind me, that I had not given in to the unbearable sorrow. I felt free. It was the first time after the liberation that I could think clearly. Maybe the

Chapter 14 / My Bleeding Heart

feeling that I am not alone did it. I had lost Fishel, but at least now I had my surviving brothers. Still, thinking of Fishel made me feel sad. I would never forget him. Raising my eyes to the sky, I pleaded, "Lord, take care of him wherever he is."

However long I will be on this Mother Earth, in my heart I will bear the scar of losing my favorite brother. I am alive, but he is gone forever. Still, he is alive in my soul for as long as I live.

Early the next morning I went to my aunt's room. "I do not have words to express my thanks to you for taking care of me," I said to her. "You are like a mother to me. With your help I recovered; I could not have done it by myself. I was too weak. I will never forget you. You gave me back hope and a belief in tomorrow. Now the time has come for me to go. I have found my brothers and I would like to join them. Together it will be easy for me to find and to build a new life. You, too, found your daughter. Soon she will be with you."

My aunt looked at me and said, "I knew that the moment would come when you would have to go. I am so happy seeing the change in you. You are young. You still have a future in front of you. May the Almighty take care of you and your brothers. I wish all of you the best."

Morris told me that my brothers were in the displaced persons camp in Feldafing, Germany, and I wanted desperately to go there to see them. But first Morris was going to Radom to meet up with a friend who was with him in the concentration camps. He asked me to go with him, and from there we would travel to Feldafing to find our brothers. Memory of my recent visit to the city was still fresh in my mind and so I was not eager to return. But I also felt that if going back to Radom was the only way I could go with Morris to Feldafing, then I would go. Henia also agreed to go with us.

Early in July 1945, the three of us left for Radom, the city that was once my home. Of the thirty-five thousand pre-war Jewish habitants, only one family survived intact—Mr. and Mrs. Den, their two sons, Moniek and Lutek, and one daughter, Hanka. Mr. Den's sister, Fajgusia Goldfarb, had also survived. There were only some one hundred other Jews in the city—single members of families who had returned to their place of birth, looking for surviving loved ones.

Again, I became sad and depressed that the once thriving Jewish community in Radom had been decimated. No sign of Jewish life remained; the places of worship were destroyed, the streets in the so-called ghetto had been obliterated. It was strange to behold the places once so familiar and now so unrecognizable, so alien.

Chapter 14 / My Bleeding Heart

A cold wind blew through my body. I knew my yesterdays were gone forever. It was so heartbreaking for me.

Morris met his friend, who wanted to travel with us to Feldafing. I could not wait to leave Poland, which now wasn't a place for survivors. It was the only country in Europe where the killing of Jews continued after the war's end. Poles in Radom and elsewhere resented their former neighbors with whom they had lived for generations knocking on doors that were once their homes. During the German occupation, some Jews had left valuables with Polish friends for safekeeping, with the understanding that it would be returned if they survived the war. Some did return money and jewelry when survivors came to reclaim them, but more Poles were less honorable. Some, in their greed, killed the returning survivors in order to keep the wealth and property they had acquired as a result of the Holocaust.

We stayed with some survivors in an apartment at 30 Zeroskiego Street. Returning to the city filled me with tears and memories of the slaughter of my family and my people. A culture that had thrived for centuries had been ruined in just a few short years. Everything was gone forever. I vowed I would never come back to this place. Only my desire to look for surviving members of my family drove me to return.

I was so sad now. My soul was tormented by the loss of my parents, my little brother Abraham, but most of all I was devastated by the loss of my brother Fishel. It had never entered my mind that he would perish. But then I was reminded that four of my brothers did survive, and at least I could look forward to being reunited with them.

It took time to secure the proper papers for the journey to Feldafing. Until then we were stuck in Radom, where hooligans roamed the streets, attacking anyone suspected of being Jewish. We walked around in groups, for safety sake. At night we stayed in our apartment, afraid to venture outside. We placed a heavy wooden table against our locked door, upon which we piled heavy wooden chairs, high to the ceiling. We hoped that the noise from the falling chairs would scare away anyone who tried to barge into our apartment. Even so, I could not sleep at night, petrified that ruffians might assault us in our beds. Only when it got lighter outside would I fall asleep, but only for a few hours.

Days passed while we made preparations to leave the city. It was for me a time both scary and profoundly sad. My sorrow was relentless; my yesterday's world was gone forever and everything in the city reminded me of the loss of those dear to my heart. Remnants of Jewish life lay everywhere in ruin, from broken monuments in Jewish cemeteries to empty lots where proud synagogues had once stood for hundreds of years. Mother Nature was taking over where once the Jewish ghetto had been. Shrubs and grass covered the empty places. It was so strange for me to see the places where I had grown up. Radom was a city without Jews. For the sake of my loved ones and my people I tried to remember the places associated with the heritage, the history of our people.

CHAPTER FIFTEEN
THE MOMENT I WAS WAITING FOR

One day, at noontime, while walking around I heard a voice from far away calling "Chaiale." I thought it was a dream, unable to conceive of anyone calling me. But there before me was a young man running in my direction. I did not recognize him. Then everything happened so quickly: He embraced me and kissed me. I pushed him away and looked strangely at him.

"Chaiale, this is me, Joseph," he said.

Startled, I began to shake, my heart beating out of control. It was a shock for me; I could not believe what I was seeing. It took a few seconds before I could get a word out. In a hoarse voice, breathing loudly, I said, "Joseph, you are here alive? I thought you had perished. You came into my life unexpectedly. In one moment you disappear and now you are back again. It is a miracle. You survived."

Holding me, he declared: "Finally, I have found you. For this moment I have been waiting and dreaming. Now I will never let you go."

My head was on fire. So many thoughts came into my mind. I had lost Fishel, my parents, and two brothers. Now Joseph had reappeared in my life. Was this the price I had to pay? Still, I could not think clearly. Joseph's voice made me happy, excited. I tried to hold myself together and not to cry for joy. And so, the moment arrived that changed my life.

For hours I walked with Joseph, relating what had happened since we were last together at the Szkolna labor camp. We shared the horror of the past few years and reminisced about the Radom of our youth. I felt something was happening to me, something intense and significant. When we parted I returned to my apartment and lay on my bed, just closing my eyes, thanking the Almighty for giving me back Joseph. "Lord, please guide me on my road back to my brothers. Take care of Joseph. You gave him back to me. Please take care of him."

Dormant feelings for Joseph now washed over me, filling my soul and my being. It awakened other emotions as well. I began to comprehend what it really meant to be free; no more being closed in, unable to move. There were no fences around me; I could now do whatever I wanted to do. I felt I was becoming a normal human being again. I realized in life I could not have everything, that I had to give up something to get something. I had lost my most precious and dear parents, and then Fishel. Was this the price I had to pay? I came to the conclusion that I couldn't change my destiny. Finally, I made my peace. I quietly prayed, "Thank you, Lord, for saving my four brothers and Joseph." I felt relaxed and happy.

The following day our travel papers arrived along with instructions on how to conduct ourselves on our way out of Poland. The most difficult and dangerous times would be at the Polish side crossing the frontier into Czechoslovakia. We were cautioned to avoid Polish groups, especially members of the National Party. Roaming around, looking for Jews departing from Poland with valuables, these brigands would rob their hapless victims, in some cases murdering them so as not to leave witnesses.

While packing for our journey, Joseph came in and told me that he had just found out that one of his aunts, Nadia Gutman, had survived and was living in Radom. She wanted to join her sister in France and asked Joseph to stay a few days to help her get ready for her trip to Paris. Turning to me, Joseph asked, "Would you stay a few days more? My aunt is sick. She needs some help. In tears, she was asking me to help her. I couldn't refuse. I promised I would stay. Please stay a few days longer so we can leave Poland together."

Morris was in the room, listening. He told Joseph, "We have already made the arrangements. We are leaving tomorrow, early in the morning. You have the whole night to think this over. You can still join us in the morning. It is up to you. We have to go."

Joseph sat and thought. Then turning to me, he said, "First, I have to talk to my aunt. Then I will decide what to do tomorrow morning." Turning to Henia and Morris, he said goodbye.

CHAPTER SIXTEEN
THE JOURNEY TO FELDAFING

It was a short night. Early in the morning Morris came to my apartment. I had hoped Joseph would show up as well. He didn't. Morris reminded us that we didn't have time to wait, that our train would be leaving in forty-five minutes. He said to me, "Chaiale, we have to leave. Don't worry. If Joseph truly loves you, he will join you in Feldafing. He knows the way." Quickly I interrupted, "Let's wait another ten minutes." Then finally, I said, "Let's go."

Up to the last minute I thought Joseph would come. Aboard the train I felt confused and conflicted. Losing my parents and Fishel had touched me deeply. Just thinking about seeing and joining my surviving brothers made me feel not so lost. When Joseph came I was happy to see him, but I had made up my mind to join my brothers. Did I do right by leaving without him? I wondered.

Morris was reading my mind and gently whispered, "Chaiale, do not worry. Joseph will come to Feldafing. When I came back to Radom looking for you I was busy and didn't have time to talk to you. Now, I have to tell you. I found out you had survived when I was with Joseph in Feldafing. When I told Joseph, he became excited and said, 'Morris, I'm going back. You brought me the news I was waiting for. Thank God Chaiale is alive. I'm lonely without her. It is so sad that Fishel didn't survive. Wherever he is, he knows about Chaiale and me. He was the one who I asked, if I survived, if I could marry your sister. His answer was she is the one who you have to ask. I never got the chance to put the question before her. Now the Almighty has given me back my life and Chaiale has also survived. The time is now for me to go and be with her. I'm leaving for Radom in the morning. I vowed I would never return to Poland, which, for me, is a graveyard. But I will return there if I can see Chaiale.'" Morris continued, "Remember, he is in love with you. Let's hope that he will be back. He will join us."

I was greatly moved by what Morris related to me. I closed my eyes as tears rolled down my cheeks.

After an entire day on the train we reached Katowice. I was astonished by what I saw: great numbers of Jewish children who had managed to survive. I couldn't comprehend where all the children had come from. I learned that some had lived with Polish families during the war. Their Jewish parents had paid a lot of money for hiding their children with the understanding that after the war the children would be given back to their parents or to some Jewish organization. Unfortunately, this did not happen in many cases. Thousands of Jewish children were never told of their parentage and remained with Polish families. Others were protected in Catholic orphanages and were raised as Christians. Their survival was a blessing, but most of them were permanently lost to Judaism.

In Katowice we met members of the *Bricha*, the Jewish Brigade. These were young men from Palestine, then under British control, who wanted to fight the Nazis. They formed the Jewish Brigade and fought as part of the British fighting forces in Europe. Because Jews faced some dangers and risks traveling in war-torn Europe, soldiers in the Brigade agreed to escort us out of Poland. After a few days in Katowice, Henia, Morris, and I, along with our military escort, were on a train leaving Poland and heading for Czechoslovakia.

Prague was a busy hub for Jewish refugees coming and going, always on the move. Some who arrived in the city in the morning left that same evening. We stayed in the city for a few days, waiting for travel papers that would allow us to go to the German frontier and then to Feldafing.

Czechs, recently freed from German oppression, had regained their country. We had freedom but without a country; stateless people with nowhere to go. But the country was hospitable to Jews, and Jewish charities and American-sponsored organizations were established to assist survivors on their way out of Poland. They set up kitchens with kosher food and provided medical help and places to sleep for us.

During the few days in Prague I worried about Joseph's safety. I slowly began to realize the feelings I had for him. I recalled the time we hid in the attic during the SS action in the small ghetto. We spoke for hours while in hiding, and I felt very comfortable in his company. It was the first time in

Chapter 16 / The Journey to Feldafing

my life that I was with some young man other than my brothers who constantly protected me. I was raised in a traditional religious Jewish household where, from the first day of her birth, a girl was always at home with her mother or with some other female family member. Never had I had the occasion to talk to someone else. There was no playing with boys. Parents made arrangements through a matchmaker for the future of their children, and so a girl met her husband for the first time at the wedding ceremony. This was the way of life for hundreds of years in Jewish communities of Eastern Europe, but in Poland, after World War I, the traditional Jewish way of life began to change.

As a young girl I did not understand the new wind blowing in our community. I was but a teenager when the Nazis invaded, thereby disrupting my normal way of life. I was just starting on my road to maturity when, in the blink of a second, I lost my freedom. I was turned into a slave waiting to be sacrificed on the altar of the Nazi empire. Romance was something that had been denied me, and now I was overwhelmed by the tenderness and affection I felt for Joseph.

After several days in Prague, we were told to get ready to leave and cross the frontier to Bavaria, Germany. I was excited over the prospect of meeting my brothers in Feldafing, but also nervous about the possible dangers that lay ahead. We would travel by train to the Czech-German frontier and then journey by foot through a forest into Germany. Members of he Jewish Brigade informed us that we would encounter Russian soldiers at the frontier who would ask us for American cigarettes. So before leaving Prague we purchased many packs of American cigarettes, which, in some places, served the same purpose as currency.

When we boarded the train we were joined by a group of other survivors, many of whom were from Radom. Again, we had protectors from the Jewish Brigade with us. We arrived at a small railroad station not far from the Czech-German frontier, where we disembarked. Detachments from the Jewish Brigade led us silently into a forest. Luckily, it wasn't hot, and the air was fresh and cool. Moving ahead, I tried not to lose contact with the people who moved very slowly in front of us. We were told not to panic when we met Russian soldiers who, we were assured, wouldn't harm us. As predicted, we encountered soldiers form the Red Army just before we reached the German border. They were very polite when they asked for cigarettes. We gladly complied and they let us cross the frontier.

Soon we reached a fence separating Czechoslovakia from the American occupation zone in Germany. A short distance on the other side of the divide some Jewish people were waiting for us. We could then breathe more easily. The danger was behind us.

Once in Bavaria, Morris said to them, "Chaiale, we are free to move around. I know the way to Feldafing. Let's not stay too long." We said goodbye to the people who trekked with us and headed for Feldafing. We traveled by train and sometimes by truck to reach our destination. Morris served as our guide, helping negotiate our way even though we had no money. Morris, knowing the German Mark was worthless, had stocked up on American cigarettes, which he now used to barter for food. He explained to me all about the abnormal way of life to which I had to get accustomed. I was grateful for his help, but I was also filled with apprehension of what awaited us in Feldafing.

We drew nearer to Feldafing, a little Bavarian town surrounded by a picturesque forest near Stamberger Lake. At one time, the area had been a vacation place for wealthy Germans. From both sides of the highway, I marveled at the many trees and the greenery. This was July, summer in southern Bavaria, with nature in full bloom. Staring outside while the truck was moving, I could not find a sign of the war that had raged so long. Small villages on the horizon were so beautiful, surrounded by trees full of fruits ready to be picked. I could see children in traditional Bavarian clothes playfully chasing their dogs. Flowers surrounded every house in such beautiful colors.

Later, while on a train, I continued to admire my surroundings as we rolled past the countryside, framed by a beautiful blue sky interrupted by wisps of clouds. I forgot where I was as I luxuriated in this radiant moment. I felt alive, free to enjoy the beauties of the natural world—and I was happy at last. I thought, it was good to be young. I relaxed. I thought about Joseph, wanting to be near him. Tired, I closed my eyes for a while. Then Morris announced, "Soon we will be in Feldafing."

When we pulled into the terminal, I got quickly down from the train. Soon we were on our way to the camp. We walked through a densely wooded area where the fresh air reinvigorated me. But I was still nervous, thinking that in but a few minutes I would be with my brothers. We reached a gate with a sign that said "FELDAFING D.P. LAGER." Entering the camp, we saw many emaciated people whose faces bore a pallid, yellowish hue. Most wore tattered clothes, although some had on American military jackets. Some wore American army boots. There were no children in the camp, for they had vanished, murdered by the Nazis, one and one-half million of them.

Chapter 16 / The Journey to Feldafing

Trembling, I looked around hoping to see one of my brothers. My heart thumped as we approached the entrance of a building. Morris turned and said, "Here is where I was living with our brothers. It will be a surprise for them to see you. I didn't let them know of our arrival." We stepped into the building and I thought I was at the Szkolna Labor Camp. There were wooden beds on both sides of a large hall and a long table in the middle of the room, just as it was in Szkolna.

Suddenly my younger brother Yakale came running out. For seconds I just stared at him, barely recognizing him. In a shaking voice I called, "Yakale, this is me, your sister, Chaiale. Don't you remember me?" As he came closer he started to cry and called, "Chaiale, Chaiale, I love you. I missed you. I'm so happy to see you."

Several seconds later Herman and Sam entered the room. What an unforgettable moment! We cried, kissed, and hugged one another. We gazed at each other in wonder. No words could describe this moment of joy. After so much time of suffering and personal tragedy, the last surviving members of the family Borenkraut were finally together.

Happiest of all was my brother Sam when he saw Henia. His eyes filled with tears of joy as he embraced her in his arms, so tight, afraid to lose her. I was touched when Henia gave Sam the sweater that I had knitted for him at Oberaltstadt. She told Sam, "We were hungry and cold in the camp, but Chaiale knitted this sweater for you. She couldn't forget you. At night I sat while your sister finished it. We waited and dreamed for the day our family would be together again."

Sam held on to her and came close to me with tears in his eyes and said, "I, too, was dreaming of this moment. I knew already about our parents, that they had perished in Treblinka. I was sure that you and Henia would survive. Both of you were young and strong. The Almighty gave me a double gift: my sister and my love, Henia. Both of you are here.

"We paid a high price for this moment," Sam continued. "We lost, besides our parents, our two brothers, Fishel and Abraham. But we will always remember our loved ones who perished. At last we survived this living hell. What is in front of us we do not know? We can only look for a happy tomorrow and pray for the best."

During the next few weeks I felt miserable. Morris was busy with his friends; Henia was happy and always with Sam. I hardly had anyone to talk to. But then I thought about Joseph. I yearned to be with him; I felt lonely without him. The worst time for me was at night lying in bed—hours and hours in the darkness, staring through the window at the heavens.

But with the stars blinking on high, slowly the light from the moon awakened in my soul a feeling of joy. I gradually came to the conclusion that life is a struggle and we have to be strong to meet its challenges—with the roses come the thorns.

One week passed after the other. September came; the summer changed to autumn. I tried to find something to do to kill the time while I waited for Joseph and helped Henia to sew some covers for our beds from the military blankets given us. But I could not stop thinking, "Would he come back? Is he all right?" I was getting nervous.

The camp where we temporarily lived was situated in the middle of a forest not far from a lake. It was an ideal place to relax. I often walked through the forest to the lake and would sit at the shore admiring this place of beauty and tranquility. I questioned how someone who grew up in this lovely part of Germany could be so full of hate. After all, it was in a beer hall in this Bavaria where the Nazis had started the dream of their so-called Thousand Year Reich.

At the end of September, I was once again passing through the camp gate during my morning walk when I heard an excited voice calling my name, "Chaiale, Chaiale." And there he was, running toward me, shouting, "Chaiale, Chaiale, I'm back." I was overwhelmed, unable to get a word out. Deep in my heart I had prayed to the Almighty, begging Him to bring Joseph back to me. And now he was here. It was very difficult for me to hold back my emotions. Speechless, frozen to the place where I stood, I stared at him, finding it difficult to comprehend that he was finally with me. I had felt so lonely since we were separated, always thinking and waiting for this moment. Now I could only gaze upon him, making sure that it was really him.

He talked quickly, without interruption, and then he abruptly stopped and handed me a package. "You can't refuse to take this," he said. "I bought it in Prague. I wish with my whole heart that Fishel could be here to share this occasion. I will always remember him. He was truly my friend. He knew how I felt about you." Tears welled up in his eyes as he continued. "One evening at Szkolna, when we left the women's barracks, I said to Fishel, 'Let's hope that we survive this hell, and if we do, I would like to marry Chaiale.'"

We entered the barracks and I called loudly, "Herman, Sam, Morris, come quickly, Joseph is back." They, too, were very happy to see him. Surrounded by my loved ones, I nevertheless wanted to get away and be alone with Joseph. We took a long walk and talked late into the night.

Chapter 16 / The Journey to Feldafing

When he left I was still nervous and full of excitement. Joseph was finally here. No more need to worry about him. Now I had my brothers and Joseph. Realizing that I couldn't be happier, I fell into a deep, satisfying sleep.

Early the next morning, Joseph came to awaken me holding a bouquet of beautiful flowers. For the next few months, every morning Joseph was at my sleeping quarters with a bundle of flowers, greeting me with a smile. With every passing day, spending time together, I started to understand him. Never before had I had the occasion to be with any men besides my brothers. Now I was with Joseph. In his company I sensed new and strange emotions welling up inside me. I had read some books about love and romance, but my life had been cut off just as I began opening my eyes. Instead. I was removed to another world, Planet Auschwitz, just Number A-24490, waiting only to starve to death or be outright killed by the Nazis. Love was a strange and wonderful thing to me. But despite my newfound joy, deep in my heart I knew that my soul was permanently scarred by what I had been through and by my grief over Fishel.

The more time Joseph and I spent together, I came to know just how close he had been to Fishel. One day while we were walking, Joseph turned to me and said, "Your brother always talked to me about you. He loved you so much." I was deeply touched. Immediately I said, "It is time to find the place where my brothers buried Fishel."

The next morning we went to Dachau. Everything was gone; the ground covered with grass. We wandered around for hours looking for the stones that Sam had used to mark the resting place of our brother. Finally, Sam recognized an area. We had found Fishel's grave. I fell to the ground, sobbing uncontrollably. I was inconsolable, awash in sorrow. Standing around the earthen mound, my four surviving brothers prayed and said *Kaddish* for my beloved Fishel.

That evening my brothers told me about the last time they had seen our brother. He was in a hospital, sick, weak and unable to walk. He told them, "I'm too weak to go on. I will stay here. Please leave me." They tried to persuade him to come with them but he insisted, "You go. I will stay here." No doubt Fishel felt that in his condition he would put his brothers in danger. He knew that they were weak from starvation and because they would have to carry him he would slow them down. I knew Fishel; he chose to stay so his brothers would have a chance to live.

CHAPTER SEVENTEEN
MY DREAMS ARE FULFILLED

Toward the end of September 1945, on a beautiful sunny day, I said to Joseph, "Let's go to the lake. I would like to show you my hiding place where I would sit for hours, waiting and praying for the moment that you would come back. You will see what a wonderful place it is. To describe it in one word, it is a paradise. It is so beautiful"

It took us no time to get there. We came to the bench where I used to sit. Then turning to Joseph, I said, "Wasn't I right?" At that moment he took my hand and looked into my eyes in and with a trembling voice he said, "I love you with all my heart. I feel I can't live without you. Will you marry me? With you at my side, wherever the Almighty will send us, I'm sure I can build a future for us."

"Yes!" I said. "This was the moment I had been waiting for. I do love you with all my heart. Wherever you will go I will go, too. I do love you."

It took about two months to arrange for a wedding. We were married at the Mayor's office in Feldafing, on November 25th, 1945, and again on March 19th, 1946, in a traditional Jewish ceremony. My four surviving brothers with their girlfriends were present, along with some new friends. Joseph arranged the wedding, paying for it with money he had received from selling property in Poland. The ceremony was held in the German Museum, the most beautiful and elegant building in Munich and one of the few structures that had survived the war. This was the moment when my dreams came true. Standing under the *chupah* (the wedding canopy), I silently prayed and thanked Him for taking care of us and giving us the opportunity to start a new life together in such an elaborate way.

Chapter 17 / My Dreams Are Fulfilled

Tears flowed from my eyes when Joseph slid the wedding ring onto my finger. In my heart I was thinking of my parents. "Mother," I whispered, "wherever you are, I want you to know I am so happy. I wish you could be here to share my happiness."

Life in Munich was difficult; the city was largely demolished and so housing was difficult to find. We found an apartment with one room and a kitchen, which we shared with other residents in the building. Joseph made a deal with a farmer who gave him a small wagon in exchange for some canned food we received in the DP camp. Each morning Joseph would load produce into the wagon that he would then haul several miles in order to sell on the streets of Munich. After a few months, he made enough money to buy fruits as well as vegetables, and the money began to roll in. Before long he built a store, selling in addition to produce, coffee and tea that he purchased in the American PX. I worked behind the counter and also served customers who came in for a cup of coffee. By 1948, we were able to buy a larger store in a train station.

CHAPTER EIGHTEEN
COMING TO TERMS WITH THE PAST

In October 1946, we were blessed with our first child, Lillian. I was not happy to have my baby delivered in a German hospital, but I had no choice. Renee, our second child, was born in 1949.

We were beginning to live comfortably, but I grew increasingly distressed living in the country that had brought the Nazis to power. I held every German I met responsible for killing my people. I desperately wanted to leave Germany, but Joseph felt differently. With the business having become more profitable, we moved to a larger apartment with two rooms and a kitchen and were living quite comfortably. But I didn't want my children to grow up in a land soaked with the blood of my people. I didn't want my children to mingle with Germans, the murderers of my parents, two of my brothers, my aunts, uncles, grandparents, and cousins. I suffered from recurring nightmares, and it was becoming increasingly impossible for me to remain in Germany. Finally, I told Joseph I would take the girls and leave, even if he didn't want to join me.

The opportunity came in June 1951, when we were informed that a temple in Southern California would sponsor us so that we could settle there. I had no idea where Pasadena was, but I was told it was a city of flowers, and flowers always made me feel good. I could not speak English, but I was willing to do anything—even scrub floors if necessary—in order to leave Germany once and for all. I knew little about Americans, other than they were the people who liberated and nourished us. So I was delighted to go to a country whose people seemed so compassionate. Happily, Joseph agreed to sell the store and start over again in the United States.

The people of Pasadena embraced us wholeheartedly. They found a place for us to live and even arranged a job for Joseph in a Formica factory, where he made tabletops. People we didn't know reached out to us, taking us around the city, showing us how to read freeway signs. I attended a city college to learn English, but I had to bring the girls with me because I had nowhere to leave them. When they got sick I could no longer attend classes; however, volunteers came to my house to continue the lessons. I will always be grateful to the people of Pasadena for their warmth and generosity in helping us to adjust to conditions in a new country.

But life was not a bed of roses for me in the city of roses. The trauma of my past continued to haunt me. When I reflect on this now, I realize that I should have seen a psychologist to help me with my problems. But in the early 1950s, I didn't know about psychology and even if I did, I couldn't afford to pay for such services. Joseph was not happy working in a factory after owning his own business in Germany. He blamed me for persuading him to leave Europe where, he said, he had everything: a good business, a nice home, and a lot of money.

I was feeling increasingly depressed when a group of survivors from Los Angeles contacted us. Several of them were from Radom, and some of them were even friends we knew in the concentration camps. We met every Sunday, discussing things we could not share with any of our other neighbors. These people became indispensable to us; we shared common memories, we spoke the same language, Yiddish, and we were all struggling to build a new life in a new country. We met often with them and they became family; we celebrated their birthdays, bar and bat mitzvahs, and weddings. I cannot imagine how Joseph and I could have adjusted to life in America without their support.

In the early 1950s, we lived in an apartment with only one bedroom where the four of us slept. Within a few months after our arrival, the country went into a steep economic recession and Joseph was laid off. Refusing to take charity, he found any work he could, doing some gardening and construction work. I took a job scrubbing floors. In 1954, our son Louis was born, and Joseph realized he had to make a real living wage. He began to sell silverware door-to-door. Even with his broken English, Joseph was pretty persuasive and soon had many customers. In the beginning I would accompany him with the children in tow, keeping records of transactions. Soon his clientele asked if they could buy other things on the installment plan and Joseph was quick to accommodate them. He purchased dried goods, bedding and other

Chapter 18 / Coming to Terms With the Past

merchandise, which he also sold door-to-door. From this work he earned enough money for a downpayment on a small house with a garage, which we transformed into a small store.

In 1958, we were blessed with our fourth child, Cecelia. Over the next decade Joseph and I kept busy raising the children and establishing ourselves in our adopted country. A few years later, Joseph bought a furniture store in downtown Pasadena, which became very successful. As time passed, we tried our best to bury our past and enjoy the good life in our adopted country.

CHAPTER NINETEEN
REVISITING THE PLACE OF OUR BIRTH

In 1973 Cecelia (or Cee Cee, as we would call her), was in the 10th grade at Pasadena High School, learning about the Holocaust in her social studies class. When the teacher realized that her parents were survivors, he invited us to speak to his class. We agreed, although Joseph was far more eager than I to recount our experiences in the Shoah. While Joseph lectured, I sat in front of the class but couldn't speak. Students would ask questions of me but all I could do was turn to my husband and hope he would answer. The wounds of my past were still too raw for me to even consider talking about what I had been made to endure.

Joseph continued to thrive in his furniture business and even tried his hand in real estate. Aside from the infrequent classroom visits, he, too, gave little thought to his life in the concentration camps. But in 1978 all that was to change. Joseph was invited to Cal Tech to listen to a lecture by a Holocaust survivor. Although reluctant, he forced himself to go, a decision that changed his life forever. The survivor was Elie Wiesel, who related experiences that resonated with Joseph in such a way that he was never the same again. He sat transfixed, eagerly consuming the speaker's every word. At the end of his speech, Mr. Wiesel announced that it was the duty of every survivor to write of his or her experiences, so that the world would never forget the greatest crime of the last century. At that point, Joseph decided he would eventually sell the business and

and return to school to learn more about the Holocaust so that he could speak more knowledgeably about it.

Any reservation he might have had about giving survivor testimony was erased by an incident involving our son Louis. In 1981, Louis was a student attending Northwestern University when he learned that a professor was planning to give a talk about the Holocaust. Naturally, his interest was aroused and he decided to attend. The speaker was Arthur Butz, an engineering professor who had written a book about the Holocaust entitled, *The Hoax of the Twentieth Century*.

At midnight, we were awakened by a phone call from Louis who sounded extremely distraught. "Dad talks about the Holocaust, but I never hear anything about it from you," he moaned. "Now a professor at my university says the Holocaust is a lie, that it never happened."

I started crying and could barely get the words out, "Oh, my son," I managed, "I have not spoken about the horrors, about the concentration camps, because I wanted to protect you. But your professor is wrong; don't believe him, don't believe him, he is trying to change history."

After I hung up I decided that I would have to do something. I survived for some reason and if I remained silent I would betray my loved ones who had died in the Nazi inferno.

I knew a man who worked at the Martyr's Museum of the Holocaust in Los Angeles. He had once asked me to serve as a docent and to share my experiences with groups visiting the museum. In 1983, I began my work at the Martyr's Museum. It was not easy for me to relate the tragic story of my life in Poland. Often, when recalling my past, I would become choked with tears and could not continue my lecture. I even wore long-sleeved blouses to cover the number tattooed on my forearm. But over time I learned to control my emotions and felt more comfortable telling my story to school children and other visitors.

In 1984, Cee Cee learned that a group was being organized for a trip to Poland and she asked if Joseph and I would join her. "I want to be part of history," she explained. "I want to see where my mother and father grew up, where they went to school, where they lived and where they suffered."

I was not interested in returning to the land of my misery, but I felt that if my youngest child wanted to see it, I had an obligation to accommodate her. We joined a group led by a Rabbi Hein Sidler and visited Krakow. From Krakow we took a bus to Auschwitz, a place I

Chapter 19 / Revisiting the Place of Our Birth

swore I would never see again. But when I arrived there it seemed as if I had never left. I could not handle reliving my darkest days; I felt I was back in time and the Germans were in control again. Even with my husband, daughter and rabbi nearby, I was frightened. I wanted to show Cee Cee the barrack where I stayed but I couldn't find it. Then I realized that the Germans had destroyed it along with the crematoria as they retreated from the Russian advance.

A guide led us to a small lake where the Nazis had scattered the ashes of the dead. I started screaming, wondering if the water contained the remains of my family. The guide then took us into an exhibit hall with showcases filled with the possessions of those who came to Auschwitz. There were hundreds, if not thousands of shoes, eyeglasses, suitcases, utensils and, most distressful, babies' teething rings. The grief felt was immeasurable, but somehow I began to feel a sense of relief. "Mom, how do you feel now?" Cee Cee asked. "Dear child," I answered, "I feel much better; I survived, I'm alive!" So the return to Auschwitz was for me a kind of therapy; I went back to my past and I came back alive.

We then traveled to Radom to visit the house in which I grew up. The street had been renamed and the balcony was gone, but I still recognized the building. Some young men saw us and spouted, "We thought they killed all the Jews. What are you doing here?" I was really frightened, but I wanted to show my daughter other parts of the city—the market, my school, the place where the Nazis made the selections. Joseph took us to the neighborhood where he grew up and the Polish people we met there were quite kind to us. They let us enter his former house and graciously showed us around. After some time, we drove back to meet up with our group and left Poland, undoubtedly for the last time.

In the years since we returned from our trip, Joseph and I have visited hundreds of classrooms to share our experiences and educate students about the Holocaust. Inspired by Elie Wiesel, Joseph made videotapes of Holocaust sites and in 1989 began to write about his past. He shared his manuscript with Professor Donald Schwartz from California State University Long Beach, who helped him publish his fist book, *Job: The Story of a Holocaust Survivor*, which appeared in 1996. Two years later, Joseph and Professor Schwartz published *The Road to Hell: Recollections of the Nazi Death March*.

Most survivor accounts have been written from the male perspective. Consequently, Joseph, Professor Schwartz and Professor John Roth of

Claremont College began to encourage me to write of my experiences. Once again, I found recalling the bitter details of my past painful and agonizing. But Joseph and Professor Schwartz persisted, so I sat down with them to tell my story.

Now that I have completed that enterprise, I feel I have fulfilled an important mission. I hope that my story will make a contribution, however modest, to teach us to be more humane than the world in which I grew up. I do not wish that anyone should be subjected to the horrors, humiliations and indignities that I was forced to suffer yet, I can also say, that I am very fortunate, not only in having come through the Nazi nightmare, but in having the chance to rebuild my life, in having the support of a loving family and a wonderful husband, and in having the opportunity to influence and educate those who must make certain that such inhumanities are never again allowed to be visited on any people.

POSTSCRIPT
MY AUNT FRANIA

My Aunt Frania took care of my every need during my stay in Zamosc, bringing me fresh fruit, rolls, sour cream and milk in the early morning and making dinner in the evening after returning from work at the hardware store. Henia and I took care of the house while Frania was away, and later helped her in the store. It was after dinner that she would sit with us, relating how she survived the war. I was transfixed by her story.

Frania had lived in Zamosc, along with her husband and three daughters, when the war broke out in 1939. They managed to endure ghetto conditions with the help of Polish friends who provided food and money. They also gave Frania a false ID, which she could use in case of an emergency.

In October 1942, the Zamosc ghetto was brutally liquidated by the German forces. By then, one daughter had escaped to Russia and another had left the ghetto and was working in a factory on the Aryan side. During the liquidation, my aunt removed her armband with the Star of David and sneaked out of the ghetto to get some food for her daughter and husband. Upon her return, she witnessed the liquidation of the Jews of Zamosc. From afar she saw the town's Jewish inhabitants shot by the SS and Ukrainian Auxiliary Police. Horrified, she ran back to her Polish friends crying, "It is time for me to get out of this place. I'm alone. My husband and little girl have been sent away by the Germans with our people. I have nowhere to go. I cannot stay here, endangering the life of your family. May the Lord take care of you. Thank you for helping me. Some day I will return and pay you back for the things which you did for me and my family."

To get out of the city she took great care to pass as a gentile. Fortunately, she hade blond hair and blue eyes and spoke fluent Polish without any accent. Leaving nothing to chance, she boarded a train wearing a big cross on her chest and under her arm was a Christian prayer book. Reasoning that it was easier to get lost in a big city, she left Zamosc for the Polish capital of Warsaw, where she assumed the appearance of a beggar. Warsaw was a crowded metropolis, full of people trying to do their best to persevere. But survival was not easy, even for Poles, as the Germans planned to transform the entire population into slaves working for the Fatherland. As a result, the streets of Warsaw were teeming with paupers just looking for handouts. Many stationed themselves at the entrances of churches, so they could plead with worshipers for food and money.

My aunt was a lost soul in Warsaw, without funds and without shelter. She slept where she could—sometimes invited into homes by strangers, sometimes on the street. It was a very hard and dangerous life, but she had no choice. Ironically, it was the Catholic churches that provided the greatest refuge for my Jewish aunt. She found a priest who gave her permission to solicit on the steps of the sanctuary. He also allowed her to wash her clothes and take care of herself in the rear of the church, but only during the warmer months. In the winter she had to clean her face and hands with snow and frequently went for weeks without washing herself. The harsh cold and rains of winter left her sick, and she often had to find refuge by sleeping on the hard wooden benches inside the church. Already familiar with Catholic liturgy, she prayed and sang along with other worshipers, with a prayer book in one hand and a cross in the other. But this, too, was not easy. At times, Polish youths taunted her by calling "*to stoy Zydowka*" ("You Jew!"), forcing her to flee to another part of the town and finding another church for safe harbor.

I began to cry as she recounted her humiliation and disgrace. Sometimes I interrupted by hugging her. I told her I knew how it felt when your heart is bleeding, when you are in pain with nowhere to turn. In my moments of torment I prayed aloud to the Creator, sometimes in Hebrew, but she couldn't afford such luxury. Her circumstances required her to swallow her misery, to conceal her suffering, and to pray to the Almighty only in silence.

For two years my aunt had to endure the shame of posing as a beggar woman, living off the magnanimity of church officials and the generosity of strangers. She also lived through the Warsaw uprising in August 1944, when the Germans destroyed the city, killing hundreds of thousands of Poles. She saw how the Nazis eradicated Polish patriots who dreamed of a democratic Poland, while the Red Army cynically watched from the other side of the Vistula. The Germans left Warsaw in ruins, liquidating almost all the inhabitants of the city. Those who did not perish were sent either to labor camps in Nazi Germany or to transit camps in Poland. My aunt was arrested and spent the remainder of the war in one such camp in eastern Poland, from where she was liberated by Russian and Polish forces in January 1945.

It was only with great difficulty that she returned to Zamosc after the war in Europe came to an end. Immediately she reconnected with her Polish friend who, true to his word, returned the hardware store that Frania had left with him years earlier. She got back her home, too, but she was alone. It was very hard for her to go on living, so it was that our finding each other came as a blessing.

AFTERWORD

Charlotte Delbo was different from Helen Freeman. She was not Polish but French. Nor was Delbo a Jew. Yet these two women are Holocaust-related sisters in more ways than one. Both of them "came back." In their special ways, each of them has also carried the word. In the pages of the book, Helen's story has been told, but her reader's reflection may be deepened by linking it with Delbo's.

Arrested for resisting the German occupation of her native France, Delbo was deported to Auschwitz in January 1943. Of the 230 French women in her convoy, she was one of the forty-nine who survived. In 1946, she began to write the trilogy that came to be called *Auschwitz and After*. Her anguished visual descriptions, profound reflections on memory and diverse writing style make it an unrivaled Holocaust testimony.

Delbo called the second part of her trilogy *Useless Knowledge*. Ordinarily we think that knowledge is useful, and it certainly can be beneficial. But Delbo showed how the Holocaust produced knowledge about hunger and disease, brutality and suffering, degradation and death that did ruin life. Among other things, Delbo's experiences proved how much words had changed, how inadequate they could be, and yet how important they are. "We came from a place," she would write, "where words had a different meaning." The words she had in mind—cold, thirsty, hungry, tired—usually say "simple things," but the Holocaust's useless knowledge gave such words meanings that were so devastating as to be incredible, if those meanings could be communicated at all to people who had not endured the Holocaust directly.

Her anguish about the useless knowledge she had acquired drove Delbo to despair. How could it not? Yet her despair was not an ending as much as a reality to be resisted as best one could. For Delbo that resistance entailed keeping memory alive. More particularly, it meant keeping alive the memory of her Holocaust sisters, those women who had been starved, beaten, and murdered—and also those who had returned, bringing with them memories that left their lives divided into before, during, and after in ways that were anything but simple because the Holocaust had changed time forever.

Writing was Delbo's way to keep memory alive. She brought to her writing a sensitive ear for dialogue, which had been tuned by work in the theater. After the Holocaust, her authorship included numerous plays, including *Who Will Carry the Word?*, written in 1966 and first staged in 1974. Delbo's instructions indicate that the play's setting is "a desolate landscape . . . a death camp in which several thousand women of all nationalities are confined." Only in relatively recent years have studies of the Holocaust focused explicitly on the experiences of women in that catastrophe. Some time before that focus became more common, Delbo called attention to these aspects of the Holocaust, as she did with the entirely female cast of *Who Will Carry the Word?*

As the play's third act begins, Denise says: "Seventy days and 'we' no longer means the same thing. Now 'we' is Gina, Francoise and myself. My sister is dead. The others are dead. All of them, all the others." The three women who remain try to keep their resistance going. "All our sentences," says Denise, "start with: 'if we come back.'" To which Gina replies: "We must say: 'when we come back.'"

The reason they must come back is to carry the word. But part of the power of Delbo's play, and the same can be said for Helen's story, is that it makes us ask: What is "the word" that must be carried? Who will carry it? And to whom will the word be carried? Clearly, the word cannot be any message that simply says "put the past behind" or "good triumphs over evil" or "there's a good reason for everything." Not only would such facile chatter trivialize, falsify, and deny the Holocaust, but, as Delbo put it, "forgetting is out of the question."

Perhaps the best one can do is just to tell what happened. But even that approach has its problems because "what happened" is so destructive, so useless. Carrying the word, Delbo knew, might be spirit-breaking, but she also understood that it must not be. Her response to this dilemma was to use her post-Holocaust life to teach and warn, to help people understand profoundly the importance of taking nothing good for granted.

Charlotte Delbo's outlook will have resonance for readers of *Kingdom of Night*, for Helen Freeman's life embodies a similar perspective. Helen is

Afterword

one who came back. In ways informed specifically by being a girl and then a woman, she knows what "useless knowledge" involves. I expect that her Holocaust memories still invite despair. But I also know that she has used her life to teach and warn, to help people understand profoundly the importance of taking nothing good for granted. I know these things not only because I have read the book that she and her loving husband, Joseph, have crafted so sensitively together, but also because Helen is a friend who teaches me and my Holocaust classes at Claremont McKenna College.

The word she carries is that we must learn to be more humane. The Holocaust nearly blotted out the word humane. Helen will not let us forget that fact. Nor will she give up insisting that we must redeem that word, restore meaning to it, so that Holocaust-related darkness does not engulf what is right and good and beautiful. Helen concludes her story with the hope that it will make a contribution in those healing directions. She has carried the word. She gives her readers good reason to do so as well.

John K. Roth
Claremont, California

GLOSSARY

A

AUSCHWITZ (Polish, Oswiecim), largest Nazi concentration and extermination camp, located 37 miles (60 km) west of Cracow. Auschwitz was both the most extensive of some two thousand concentration and forced labor camps, and the largest camp at which Jews were exterminated by means of poison gas.

AMERICAN GI – American soldier.

ADL – Anti-Defamation League of B'nai B'rith, fights against racial hate and injustice; a Jewish organization.

Arbeitslager – (German word) labor-camp.

Antisemitism – Prejudice against and fear of Jews, either religiously or racially, or both.

Aktion – (German) operation involving the rounding up and deportation of Jews from the ghettos or urban centers to death camps.

B

Blitzkrieg – (German) Term used to describe the intense German military campaign which resulted in swift victories.
Bahnhof – (German) railroad station.

Blockelder – (German) block supervisor.

Bar Mitzvah -(Hebrew) Religious confirmation for a boy at age 13.

Burgermeister – (German) mayor of a city.

Bug River – a river running north to south in Poland that divided Germany and Soviet forces after the Non-Aggression Pact of 1939.

C

Challah – (Hebrew) special braided bread for Sabbath meals.

Cheder – (Hebrew) Hebrew school.

Cyna brothers – the only ones who escaped from the "Death March" in 1944.

D E

Dachau – death camp in Bayern Germany.

Diaspora – term for the dispersion of Jews all over the world after the destruction of the Temple in Israel.

Einsatzgruppen – (German) mobile units of the German Security Police that followed the German armies into the Soviet Union in 1941. These SS units were in charge of killing the Jewish population. They also murdered Soviet commissars, Gypsies and mental defectives. Most victims were shot and buried in mass graves.

Extermination camps – death camps, killing centers. These were the camps built specifically for the mass killing of Jews and in some camps Gypsies, Russian prisoners of war, and others. Most of the corpses were then burned in crematoriums or in open fields. Extermination is a Nazi word, something that is done to rodents, not people.

F G

Feldafing – DP camp in Bayern, West Germany.

Glossary

Glinice ghetto – (suburb of Radom) where a small ghetto was established, March 1941 in Radom

Goy – (Yiddish) a non-Jew.

Gestapo – (German) The Secret State Police of the Third Reich.

H
Hasid – (Hebrew) An ultra-observant Jew dedicated to a religious observance founded in Jewish mysticism.

K

Kaddish – (Hebrew) Jewish prayers recited by mourners for the deceased.

Kapo – Jewish foremen, assigned by Germans at the concentration camps.

Kielce – a city in Poland. After World War II, 42 Jewish survivors, with the assistance of the local Polish constabulary, were killed by antisemitic Poles.

L

Lagerfuerer – (German) German official in charge of a death camp.

Lagerelder – (German) supervisor over *kapos* in the death camps.

M

Majdanek – death camp in Poland.

Mein Kampf – (German) *My Struggle*—Hitler's vision of the National-Socialist ideology and political program for the future Nazi Empire, written by Hitler while in Landsberg prison.

Mengele, Josef – German doctor in charge of the selection process in Auschwitz, and of medical experiments on inmates; also known as the "Angel of Death."

P R

Pentz garden – a place in Radom where the Nazis buried thousands of Jewish inhabitants massacred at the liquidation of the city in 1942.

Pogrom – attack on Jews by the local population.

Peretza Street – a name of a street in Radom.

Rynek – a street in Radom.

S

Siddur – a Hebrew prayer book.

Shul – (Yiddish) a Jewish house of worship.

Szpitalna Street – a street in Radom where the SS formed a ghetto that the Nazis liquidated in July 1944.

Szydlowiecz – a small town in Poland

Staatslose Jüde – (German) a Jew without a country.

T V

Tallit – (Hebrew) Ritual prayer shawl with four corners, symbolizing the 613 laws of the Torah.

Tzedaka – (Hebrew) charity.

Volksdeutsch – (German) a German living outside of Germany.

W Y

Waffen – (German) weapons

Warszawa – Warsaw, the capital of Poland

Wolanow – a small town about 12 miles from Radom.

Wehrmacht – (German) Army

Yeshiva – (Hebrew) a religious school for boys studying Talmud.

Glossary

Z

Zamlynia – a street in Radom.
Zeromskiego Ulica – (Polish) the main street in Radom.

SOURCES

Bauer, Yehuda and Nili Keren. *A History of the Holocaust.* Scholastic Publishing, 2001
Berkovits, Eliezer. *Faith After the Holocaust.* KTAV, 1990.
Carroll, James. *Constantine's Sword: The Church and the Jews – A History.* Houghton Mifflin, 2001.
Czerniakow, Adam. Raul Hilberg, Stanislaw Staron and Josef Kermisz, eds. *The Warsaw Ghetto Diary: Prelude to Doom.* Stein & Day, 1979.
Cornwell, John. *Hitler's Pope: The Secret History of Pius XII.* Viking, 1999.
Feig, Konnilyn G. *Hitler's Death Camps.* Holmes & Meir, 1981.
Fein, Helen. *Accounting for Genocide: National Response and Jewish Victimization During the Holocaust.* Free Press, 1979.
Furet, Francois. *Unanswered Questions: Nazi Germany and the Genocide of the Jews.* Knopf, 1989.
Grobman, Alex and Daniel Landes, eds. *Critical Issues of the Holocaust: A Companion to the Film Genocide.* Simon Wiesenthal Center, 1983.
Gutman, Israel. *Encyclopedia of the Holocaust.* Macmillan, 1989.
Koehl, Robert Lewis. *Black Corps: The Structure and Power Struggles of the Nazi SS.* University of Wisconsin, 1983.
Korczak, Janusz. *Ghetto Diary.* Holocaust Library, 1978.
Lifton, Robert J. *Nazi Doctors: Medical Killing and the Psychology of Genocide.* Macmillan, 1986.
Lipson, Alfred, ed. *The Book of Radom: The Story of a Jewish Community in Poland Destroyed by the Nazis.* United Radom Relief for U.S. and Canada, 1963.
Meed, Vladka. *On Both Sides of the Wall: Memoirs from the Warsaw Ghetto.* Beit Lohamei Haghettaot, 1973.

Rittner, Carol and John K. Roth, eds. *From the Unthinkable to the Unavoidable: American Christian and Jewish Scholars Encounter the Holocaust.* Greenwood Publishing, 1997.

Tetens, T. H. *Know Your Enemy.* Society for the Prevention of World War III, 1944.

Tokayer, Marvin and Mary Swartz, *Fugu Plan: The Untold Story of the Japanese and the Jews During World War II.* Paddington Press, 1979.

Wiesel, Elie. *And the Sea is Never Full : Memoirs 1969- .* Knopf, 1999.

_____*All Rivers Run to the Sea: Memoirs.* Schocken, 1996.

_____*Where are the Children? Conversations in Germany with Herb Brin.* Jonathan David, 1991.

World Jewish Congress. *Black Book: The Nazi Crime Against the Jewish People.* Jewish Black Book Committee, 1946.

Wyman, David S. *The Abandonment of the Jews: America and the Holocaust, 1941-1945.* Knopf, 1984.

www.ingramcontent.com/pod-product-compliance
Lightning Source LLC
Chambersburg PA
CBHW021129300426

44113CB00006B/353